AF573744

PRIORIES AND ABBEYS OF ENGLAND

Books by the same author:

Castles of England

Odd Aspects of England

Customs and Traditions of England

London in Colour

Inns and Villages of England

A Guide to English Country Houses

The Shell Book of Exploring Britain

PRIORIES AND ABBEYS OF ENGLAND

Garry Hogg

David & Charles : Newton Abbot

Special Edition for the
Readers Union
Group of Book Clubs

ISBN 0 7153 5533 3

Set in 11 on 13pt Plantin
and printed in Great Britain by
W J Holman Limited Dawlish
for David & Charles (Publishers) Limited
South Devon House Newton Abbot Devon

CONTENTS

ACKNOWLEDGEMENTS

The author acknowledges with thanks permission to use plates 13, 17, 19, 23, 29, 31, 37, 41, 47, 49, 51, 53, 55, 63, 65, 67, 69, 71, 73, 77, 83, 87, 89, 91, 93, 95, 99, 101, 103, 105, 107, 109 kindly supplied by the Department of the Environment; plates 11, 15, 57, 61, 75, 79 kindly supplied by the British Tourist Authority; plates 33, 39, 45, 59, 85, 97 kindly supplied by Messrs Barnaby Picture Library; the following plates kindly supplied by: plate 21, Country Life; plate 25, Russell Adams; plate 27, Montagu Motor Museum, Beaulieu; plate 35, The Friars, Aylesford; plate 43, J. A. Entwistle; plate 81, Aerofilms Ltd.

FOREWORD

The number of religious houses, or monastic establishments, that have survived to this day in a greater or lesser degree of preservation since their foundation in or about the era of the Norman Conquest runs into two or three hundred at least. They were founded as monasteries to house a community of monks. Some of these were elevated to the status of abbey under the rule of an abbot; or their status might be slightly inferior to this, in which case they would be known as priories, ruled over by a prior. Generally speaking, a priory was likely to be an offshoot of some neighbouring (or even distant) abbey. The point is made to emphasise the fact that there have always existed shades of meaning among the terms used; these tend to overlap, and so induce confusion. A convent, for instance, is ordinarily thought of as synonymous with a nunnery, though in fact it could house either monks or nuns; the term conventual buildings is employed *pari passu* with monastic buildings.

The full story of the founding of these priories and abbeys is fascinating, but it is too long to recount in any detail here. Very briefly, monks, as we think of them, were the medieval descendants of a tradition started in the early centuries of the Christian era by hermits who isolated themselves from their fellow men in order to live a spartan life of prayer and fasting. The sites selected were always in remote, inhospitable regions, often on the east and south sides of the Mediterranean. St Simeon Stylites was one of these: he spent no less than thirty-seven years of his life on the top of a pillar in the Syrian desert. Later on, these solitaries, or monks (the very word comes from a Greek word meaning 'alone'), began to group themselves into small, ascetic communities which spread northwards and westwards across Europe by way of Italy and France to Ireland, and thence to England.

In due course, under the influence of certain saints and other dominating factors, there came into being a number of orders. Each of these differed from the others in certain respects, but all of them were fundamentally Christian, and the members of the orders were men dedicated to the worship of their God and the practice of the faith as understood by them.

The best known of the orders, the one whose signature is left most widespread upon the land, were the Benedictines. As their name implies, they followed the rules laid down by St Benedict, who founded a monastery in Italy in the year AD 529. It is no exaggeration to state that the Benedictine Rule became the basic tenet of all medieval monasticism, though the other orders in the course of time were to evolve their own interpretations of this.

Almost equally well known were the Cistercians, who derived their name from the Abbey of Cîteaux in France, founded in the latter part of the eleventh century by, as it happens, an English abbot. Generally speaking, theirs was a sterner, more ascetic rule than that of St Benedict. The Carthusians also took their name from a French town, in this case Chartreuse. Today we may inevitably associate that name with a delectable liqueur, but in fact the Carthusians were an even more ascetic order than the Cistercians. In their Charter Houses they lived a life of almost complete solitude; each man had his own cell for sleep and study; he wore a hair shirt as a constant reminder (as if he needed this!) that life meant hardship and pain. He was not allowed to speak with, or even see, the lay-brother who brought to his cell his meagre daily ration of food and water. The Carthusians shared this bleak way of life with the Trappist monks, a very strict order that broke away even from the ascetic Cistercians, and had imposed upon them the strict rule of absolute silence.

Another order was that of the Cluniacs, whose name derived from the little French town of Cluny. The majority of their establishments were small, and their order never came to be recognised as widely as that of the Benedictines and Cistercians. Two other orders were the Augustinians and the Premonstratensians. The first of these—known also as Austin Canons or, because of their robes, Black Canons—took their way of life from the rule of St Augustine. It is clear from contemporary records that they lived an easier life and spent their time in greater comfort than the monks who belonged to other monastic orders. The Premonstratensians, who derived their name from the small French town of Prémontre, wore white robes, and came to be known as White Canons. Their order, like that of the Cluniacs, never flourished in England in the way that the Benedictine and Cistercian orders did.

There are not many monasteries, in the familiar, accepted sense, to be found in England today. Perhaps the Benedictine foundations of Ampleforth and Downside come first to mind, but this may well be because of the fine boys' schools so closely identified with them. Aylesford Priory, a Carmelite establishment more usually known as 'The Friars' from its medieval tradition which sent men out into the highways and byways to preach and heal and convert rather than restricting them to life within a monastery's precinct, flourishes again today after many vicissitudes. Buckfast Abbey and Prinknash Abbey are entirely modern religious houses, the one completed and the other fast nearing completion, though they stand on sites that have had monastic associations down the centuries.

When we use the words priory or abbey, we are almost invariably conjuring up in our minds the noble and often hauntingly beautiful remains of some great religious house of yesteryear; one of those founded soon after the Norman Conquest and in which building continued during the centuries immediately following the consecration of the first church—quite possibly on a site that was already hallowed because of some earlier chapel or shrine that had been erected there centuries before and, because it had been built of timber and wattle, had perhaps long since disappeared.

Fifty of these priories and abbeys are briefly described and illustrated in the pages that follow. They necessarily vary a great deal in quality and character, in the impact they may be expected to have upon the visitor, especially when he comes upon them for the first time. Some of these are no more than majestic ruins: stupendous arches that once contained the great east window or helped to support the crossing tower; soaring buttresses that once served to strengthen nave or transept walls; massive but crumbling walls that once contained chancel or chapel or chapter house, frater or dorter or abbot's lodging. These are all the more impressive for rising from well-tended greensward. Their settings vary a great deal, too. There is the dramatic beauty of Whitby Abbey, poised on its headland; there is the magic of Lindisfarne on Holy Island, girt by the waters of the North Sea save for a causeway that is negotiable for only part of every twenty-four hours. How perfectly these contrast with, for example, the pastoral setting of Tintern on the banks of the Wye in Monmouthshire, or Fountains in the heart of Skelldale, or Rievaulx in Ryedale in Yorkshire, or Glastonbury, serene on the level Somerset plain.

Others survive in different form. In Malmesbury, for instance, in Wymondham and in Crowland, the abbey church is in use to this day, resuscitated or rehabilitated from the ruins left there after Henry VIII's harsh Act of Dissolution. Again, though the abbey church may have vanished, portions of the old conventual buildings have been put to appropriate use once more after centuries of neglect. In Battle Abbey, for instance, the former prior's lodging and adjacent buildings now house a girls' school; and Whalley Abbey now serves as a religious conference centre—a most appropriate metamorphosis.

There are stories enshrined in all these hallowed piles of stones, however derelict and unpromising they may seem at first sight. In the following pages the text facing each photograph consists of no more than the bare bones of each story; enough, it is hoped, to stimulate curiosity. That curiosity can be readily satisfied by perusal of the guidebooks that are to be obtained at most if not all of these sites. And the guidebook material can be amplified at will by referring to the many comprehensive studies that have been made of the individual sites. Many of these contain engravings that show what the priory or abbey looked like at successive periods of its existence; others contain 'artists' impressions' based on antiquarian research by experts down the years. Often this research has enabled the authorities to set out the ground-plan of the church and its ancillary buildings in lines of stone on the turf in such a way that one can see at a glance the original layout of these places that were planned and built so long ago and with such loving care and industry. Glastonbury is an example of this; Michelham is another, and Beaulieu yet another.

Finally, the greater number of these priories and abbeys are to be found located in regions of such scenic beauty that these alone—quite apart from the monastic treasures they enshrine—more than justify the time and effort involved in going in search of them. They, and the many others that have had to be omitted here, remain a moving, even a haunting, reminder of yet one more aspect of the heritage of tradition and beauty that we are fortunate enough to possess.

G.H.

Groombridge, Sussex.

Berkshire

ABINGDON ABBEY (Benedictine)

It was the abbey's misfortune that it stood so close to the Thames, for after the Dissolution, Henry VIII's clerk-of-works proceeded to dismantle wholesale all those monastic buildings whose stone was in good condition. This included the church itself. A flotilla of barges carried the stone downstream to London, to serve what purposes His Majesty might choose to decree. So, today, you will search the lovely, restored precinct of the abbey in vain for its major conventual buildings: for the cloister walks, the frater and parlour, dorter and chapter house and library and, on the west side, the abbots' lodgings and kitchen. Their site has been ascertained; but the stone that was the abbey's glory seven centuries ago has now been dispersed so widely that no one can say what buildings it has since comprised.

This, however, is certainly not to suggest that there is nothing here to remind us of the glory Abingdon once knew. There is still the splendid main gateway, to be found between the very ancient St Nicholas Church on one side and the equally ancient Hospital of St John on the other. These must not be confused with the abbey church and infirmary, both long since vanished. The church was built in the twelfth century for the spiritual welfare of those who were the tenants of the extensive properties owned by the abbey; the hospital was to serve their physical needs. And it was eventually to become Abingdon's Guildhall.

Passing through this fine gateway you would formerly have been heading for the west end of the abbey church. Bear right, however, and even today you will be approaching a range of domestic buildings that miraculously escaped cannibalisation and, thanks largely to the Friends of Abingdon Abbey, are in a splendid state of preservation and are indeed almost without parallel in other abbey precincts. They lie along the mill stream, once a vital adjunct to the community throughout the abbey's long history. Here is the old granary; adjacent to it is the checker-hall where the abbey's business was transacted and accounts settled. It possesses one of the finest thirteenth-century chimneys in England. Beyond this comes the long gallery, open sided and with a most impressive timber roof. Buildings such as these convey a curiously strong impression of what life must have been like in those far-off days.

Cumberland

LANERCOST PRIORY (Augustinian)

(Off A69, 2 miles north-east of Brampton)

This is one of the few ancient foundations of which the church is in use to this day. The priory was founded in 1166 by Robert de Vaux. It lies on the north bank of the River Irthing, and Hadrian's Wall runs across the north side of its precinct. Stone from this Roman fortification was used in its building—one in the south-west corner of the cloister bears the mark: C CASSI PRISCI. This form of 'cannibalisation' was balanced centuries later when stone from the priory was filched for farm buildings round about.

The site, though, was unhappily chosen. It lay virtually on the Scottish Border, and was thus in the direct line of skirmishing parties from both sides. The English forces frequently billeted themselves with the canons while recouping their strength—at enormous cost to the community; the Scots frequently raided the priory to smoke out their enemies—and took the opportunity to ravage the place at the same time. Over and over again in the late thirteenth and early fourteenth centuries the priory suffered major damage. In 1296, after locking 200 children in Hexham Church and burning them alive, the Scots came west to Lanercost, burned out the cloister and some of the surrounding buildings and terrorised the canons. Later, Robert the Bruce visited the priory and severely punished the canons whom he believed to have supported Edward I. Later still, King David II of Scotland descended on them, ransacked the buildings for spoil, and viciously desecrated the church itself. The place seemed doomed. At the Dissolution, Henry VIII sent the Duke of Norfolk to Lanercost with express instructions 'without pitie or circumstance to cause all the canons that be in anywise faultie to be hanged without further delaye'.

Not surprisingly, little survives today apart from the remains of the cellarium beneath the now-vanished frater. But the church itself still stands proud and in use. In 1740 the crumbling east end (which is still well in evidence) was sealed off at the west end of the crossing; the nave was re-roofed and otherwise extensively rehabilitated. Congregations nowadays enter by the noble west door which dates back to the year 1220. The remainder of the priory church, beyond the newly-built east wall, still has dignity, not least because of the layout of its tower and transepts, though the remainder of the priory buildings are but ghosts upon the surrounding turf.

Devonshire

BUCKFAST ABBEY (Benedictine)

(Off A38, 2 miles south of Ashburton)

To penetrate this quiet corner of the Dart Valley is to be brought face to face with a modern miracle: a Benedictine abbey in all its glory eight centuries after its foundation. The story behind it has the romance of a legend; yet it is all true.

In 1882 one of a small group of French monks who had settled here broke his hoe while gardening. Examination showed that he had not hit virgin rock, but part of the base of a wall. Excited by the find, the small community set to work, and within a year had laid bare the foundations of what records proved to have been an abbey established on the site in 1018, during the reign of King Canute. Records told how the original buildings had gradually disintegrated; how after the Dissolution they had passed into various hands; and how, early in the nineteenth century, one Samuel Berry had used what remained of them to build himself a pseudo-Gothic mansion. It was this mansion in which the French monks took up residence in 1882. And now for the miracle.

Encouraged by the chance find, and under the inspiration of the great Abbot Anscar Vonier, the community, greatly daring, resolved to rebuild the monastery on its original foundations, and by their own unaided labour. Brother Peter was despatched to France and apprenticed to a master-mason. He returned, qualified as a master-mason himself, and set about instructing a few of his brethren. Meanwhile, funds were raised for the purchase of stone and other basic materials. On 5 January 1907, the first stone was laid. Thereafter, for a quarter of a century, the monks laboured, in all weathers, from dawn to dark. No more than six could be spared from the routine activities of the monastery, but such was their dedication and ardour that by 1932, only twenty-five years after the laying of the foundation stone, the Abbey Church of St Mary, Buckfast, could be consecrated. And in the following years the great abbey itself was completed. Abbot Anscar Vonier, whose inspiration it had been, just lived to see the scaffolding removed, and then, his mission accomplished, died.

Buckfast Abbey, as we see it today, is a Benedictine monastery standing on the foundations of an eight-centuries-old Cistercian monastery; it was built, as the medieval monasteries were built, by monks turned craftsmen, labouring joyously in the worship of their God.

Co Durham

FINCHALE PRIORY (Benedictine)

(Off A1, 3 miles north of Durham)

Few saints can have had a more extraordinary early life than St Godric—'Guderic, a pirate from the Kingdom of England'—an adventurous and restless mariner and trader by the time he was twenty but with, as a contemporary records, always an urgent ambition to become a hermit and lead a life of isolated contemplation. Interspersed with his voyages were pilgrimages to such shrines as that of St Iago da Compostella in north-west Spain. For a while he shared a hermit's cell, and in a vision learned that he should thenceforward live solitary at Finchale, in a crook of the River Wear.

Like the first monks at Fountains Abbey, he lived rough to begin with; then he built a wooden hut and a tiny chapel dedicated to the Virgin Mary. His reputation for stark living and sanctity spread; countless pilgrims visited him where he lived, clad in a hair shirt and, strangely, a coat of chain-mail, until his death in 1170 at the remarkable age of 105.

Almost immediately after Godric's death a monastery was founded on the site. Godric, now canonised, lay in a tomb on the north side of the presbytery, known also as the Chapel of St John Baptist. He must have been a very small man, even by the standards of the day, for the tomb (which may still be seen) was hollowed out of a single block of stone and its inside length is barely more than five feet.

The remains of the church show that it was surprisingly large considering that Finchale was designed to have a prior and only four monks, with additional accommodation for four monks from the neighbouring Durham mother-church who were to visit Finchale for three-week rest-periods on a carefully devised rota. Here, as so often, the quire and presbytery and transepts were more ambitiously conceived than the nave. Much of this, together with the north wall of the nave, dates from the thirteenth century, though the aisles were constructed later. Unusually, the frater was separated from the kitchen that served it, by the monks' dorter, and the reredorter was unhappily placed against the kitchen itself. The frater is one of the best preserved of the monastic buildings here (unlike the Cistercian house at Buildwas, where it has been lost). But the saint's bones have long since vanished from the coffin.

ST BOTOLPH'S PRIORY (Augustinian)
(In Colchester)

An ancient site in an ancient city. For this is Camulodunum, the Romans' base on the River Colne; remains of the Roman walls, and the Balkerne Gate, testify to this. On the site of the priory, centuries earlier, there was an Anglo-Saxon church, serving a small community of monks. In the eleventh century one Norman, a man from Kent, urged this community to join one of the recognised religious orders, and so was founded, in AD 1100, the first Augustinian priory in England. Being the first, it was granted certain major privileges. Among these, it was to have absolute authority over all other Augustinian houses that might later be established in the country, with the right to check and punish misdemeanors. At its foundation, this community consisted of Prior Ainulf and twelve canons: a figure symbolising Christ and His twelve apostles.

The priory, though, was never large enough to attain prosperity and maintain it. The material of which it was built consisted largely of flint, intermixed with the standard thin Roman tile-like brick, filched from the massive Roman walls, for there was no true building-stone readily to hand. The crumbling west front and the great north wall of the nave—virtually all that has survived—reveal at once the impressive massiveness and the essential weakness of this building material, at least as utilised in the twelfth century. The sturdy round pillars (of which a few remain) support some lofty round-headed arches, but the effect comes somewhat strangely on the eye. Perhaps these disparate materials are not truly married.

In the mid-seventeenth century, Colchester came under siege. Though it is believed that the priory until that time was in a fair state of preservation, it fell victim to heavy gunfire as it was suspected of sheltering the defendants. When the siege ended, 'the parish officers, to prevent its total demolition, took the laudable resolution of enclosing and locking up the priory. This permitted weeds and shrubs to sprout among the mouldering walls, a circumstance which adds greatly to the beauty and solemnity of the scene.' May be; but among the weeds and shrubs was ivy, and this in all probability did as much damage over succeeding years as the gunfire had done in a few hours. St Botolph's is the poorer for those two forms of aggression.

Essex

ST OSYTH'S PRIORY (Augustinian)

(Off B1027, 4 miles west of Clacton)

Of the ancient buildings, founded in the twelfth century on a site hallowed by St Osyth, martyred daughter of the first Christian king of East Anglia and abbess of a small nunnery in the mid-seventh century, little remains today. You go in search of them through what is almost certainly the most magnificent gatehouse in England. Built in 1475, it is a supreme example of East Anglian flushwork: local flint set in perpendicular panels within frames of ashlar, the whole crenellated and pierced by a great central gateway for wheeled traffic to and from the monastery and a pair of lesser gateways, equally finely proportioned, for pedestrians. Great half-octagonal towers, of the same flushwork, flank the doorways. Inset in these (and one of them still visible) are two Beggars' Windows, through which pilgrims and the needy could help themselves to the food laid out for them.

Flanking the gatehouse are the east and west blocks, or wings. In one fireplace that has been well preserved there is a small, unusual and very interesting feature: a recess in the hearth wall in which that vital commodity, salt, used to be stored to be kept dry.

On the other side of the gatehouse you come to the site of the now-vanished abbey church. A topiary garden now occupies the site of the cloister, on the north side of the church. Beyond this is the site of the frater, with the cellarer's range to one side and on the other the Chapel of St Osyth, which was originally the monks' dorter. Against it is the splendidly proportioned Abbot's Tower, or D'Arcy Tower, built by Lord D'Arcy when, after the Dissolution, the property fell into his hands. As a monarch's vice-chamberlain he was a wealthy man, and much of what is to be seen here is evidence that he laid out his money intelligently and well. Standing on the great lawn, you may look back on the inner face of that superb gatehouse and adjoining wings and, in the opposite direction, at the buildings erected by the D'Arcys in later centuries. Beneath your feet are the foundations of the abbey church, and much of the stone from which these fine buildings were constructed no doubt came from its vanished walls. This corner of Essex is a quiet one at any time; within these precincts you will find an ageless serenity safeguarded into this turbulent century by this memorable gatehouse.

Gloucestershire

HAILES ABBEY (Cistercian)

(Off A46, 3 miles north-east of Winchcombe)

This was one of the last houses of the order to be established in England, more than a hundred years after the first of them at Waverley, in Surrey. The story of its founding is a romantic one. In 1242 the Earl of Cornwall, brother to Henry III, narrowly escaped disaster at sea; he vowed that if his life were spared he would found and endow an abbey in thanksgiving. He was saved, and the king granted him the manor of Hailes so that he could fulfil his vow. And there, in 1246, twenty monks and ten lay-brothers from Beaulieu Abbey established a monastic community.

Its early decades were uneventful, but in 1270, the earl's second son, Edmund, presented to the abbey a phial of the Holy Blood 'warranted genuine by the Patriarch of Jerusalem'. A shrine was swiftly constructed to contain it, and then an unusual circlet of five chapels was built, with an ambulatory, at the east end of the presbytery, half-surrounding the shrine. Very soon, Hailes Abbey had become one of the most important centres of pilgrimage in England, and its fame endured until the Dissolution. Then the phial of alleged Holy Blood was removed to London, where the Bishop of Rochester publicly declared that its contents were in fact 'honey clarified and coloured with saffron, as has been evidently proved before His Majesty the King and his Council'! (The 'guarantor' of this phial in due course became Pope Urban IV.)

The site of Hailes Abbey is a beautiful one, on the western fringe of the Cotswolds; it is lavishly framed on three of its four sides with great banks of massed trees enclosing the level sward. But there is relatively little to see today, though excavations continue and what has been revealed suggests a spacious array of monastic buildings. Such features as may be seen, notably the arches of the chapter house and cloister, are beautiful not least because they are composed of the incomparable oolitic limestone of the region, while the blue lias has been used for many of the free-standing shafts. It is disappointing—and strange too—that the buildings of so late a foundation should have survived into this century so much less well than many of those founded so much earlier than Hailes; but this abbey is worth a leisurely visit if only to visualise it as it must have been, within its magnificent frame of trees.

Gloucestershire

PRINKNASH ABBEY (Benedictine)

(Off B4070, 8 miles south-west of Cheltenham)

Prinknash (pronounced Prinish) differs from every other abbey in the country: at the time of writing it is still uncompleted, scaffolding clings to some walls, builders' equipment is on the site; it is thus newer even than Buckfast, and is as yet a dream barely fulfilled—though a dream rich indeed in promise.

Its story is a strange one. Prinknash Park has been a royally-approved monastic hunting-ground for centuries; Edward III granted the right of 'free warren' there, and the abbot's privileges were confirmed in 1397 by Richard II. The link between Gloucester Abbey and this place was at once close and unsatisfactory, at least so far as the order was concerned, though just before the Dissolution, Abbot Parker had adapted the hunting-lodge as a residence for the abbots of Gloucester. Thenceforward, for many empty years the place was deserted until, by a happy chance, it was offered as a gift to the dispossessed Benedictine monks of Caldey Island, off the South Wales coast. In 1928 an advance party of these monks left Caldey and began the long and arduous task of making the place a fit home for their community to live and work and worship in. Others soon followed. Money was sought, and forthcoming. Just before the outbreak of World War II the foundation-stone was laid by Cardinal Hinsley. Plans for a monastic building that was to have the status of an abbey were drawn up. For more than thirty years now, work on the site has been in progress—work that is now within an ace of completion to the glory of God. There is an echo here, of course, of the story of Buckfast, consecrated nearly forty years ago.

One outstanding feature of the monks' way of life is their adherence at Prinknash to St Benedict's saying: 'They are more truly monks when they live by the labour of their hands'. This labour, with its reminder that *laborare est orare,* is emphasised here in the beautiful, often inspired pottery produced by these craftsmen. It is just one of the many occupations of these dedicated men that knit the community together. Incidentally it earns money that enables them to pay for additions to their buildings that might not otherwise ever have been attained. These new buildings, too, incorporate the original one, the former hunting-lodge that became the residence of abbots in their heyday when they enjoyed the sunshine of monarchal patronage.

Hampshire

BEAULIEU ABBEY (Cistercian)

(Off B3054, 10 miles south of Southampton)

Because this forms part of a great ducal estate, that of Lord Montagu of Beaulieu, it has been cherished, and so has survived better than many others that date back also to the earliest years of the twelfth century. Generations of the present duke's ancestors have repaired and restored what was damaged both before and after the Dissolution. Though certain portions have now been again put to use, this has been done intelligently and with discretion. The result is that the visitor here obtains a clearer impression of the layout and purpose of the monastic buildings than he could elsewhere.

The original lay-brothers' dorter has been skilfully restored, and is now in fact used as a restaurant; apart from its fittings, it is substantially as it was seven centuries ago. The Outer Gatehouse—a feature of most such foundations—is in a fine state of preservation and today fulfils its original function. One interesting and most valuable feature at Beaulieu is a scale-model reconstruction of the abbey church and buildings as they are believed to have been in their heyday; it is well worth examining with care before setting out to locate the individual remains *in situ*.

The north and east sides of the cloister have survived well (with a little help); you can see the sequence of pointed arches leading to the door by which the silent monks processed into the church. You can examine the door by which they entered the frater, with its beautiful scrollwork hinges. The frater, incidentally, is now the parish church, and a fine view of it can be obtained through the remaining arches of the part-vanished chapter house. Another feature to have survived nearby is rarely found elsewhere: it is the flight of so-called night steps, the stone stairs by which the monks, barefoot or in felt slippers, descended from their dorter in the east range for a series of brief services that continued from two o'clock in the morning onwards. Yet another unusual feature is the asymmetrical doorway by which the lay-brothers entered the church from the west range, a lowlier portal than that reserved for the monks themselves. Most certainly, Beaulieu offers a simpler introduction to the idea of the religious house than any other in the country; if conditions permitted, this, surely, would be the one to visit at the outset.

Hampshire

NETLEY ABBEY (Cistercian)

(Off A3025, 5 miles south-east of Southampton)

Its name in Domesday was Letelie. Popular (and perhaps partisan) etymology held that this was a corruption of *Laetus Locus*, the Joyous Place, and early references to this thirteenth-century abbey frequently bestow this name upon it. It may not rank among our greatest abbeys but, tree-surrounded, on level ground with a slope north-eastwards and a wide view of sparkling Southampton Water to the south-west, it certainly seems to offer some justification for that descriptive epithet.

Netley was a relatively late foundation, and so has rather less history than many other religious houses. It shares, of course, one historic moment with all its fellows, of whatever order: the Dissolution put an end to its career as an abbey, but not entirely to its career. Both site and abbey buildings (including the church) were made over to the Marquis of Winchester. Wilfully ignoring its claim to respect, he proceeded to convert not only the ancillary buildings but part of the church itself into a mansion. As such, it was used for a century and a half. Then, unexpectedly, its current owner dismantled it and sold much of the massive fabric as building material. The stonework of the north transept was removed wholesale and used to construct a sham ruin, or 'folly', in Cranbury Park, not far distant.

Oddly, it may well be that the marquis's mansion helped to preserve the fabric that he had not wholly incorporated; furthermore, the dismantling, in 1700, was carried out with some care. The result is that more of the abbey survives than might be expected. There is still sufficient remaining of the presbytery and south transept to give a fair idea of the scope of the original church. The north side of the nave is later than the south side, and there is, in the south-west corner, an unusual form of entrance designed for the lowlier lay brethren: an oblique, constricted passage in strong contrast to the main doorway in the west front. A small but telling detail.

The location of the refectory shows imagination, for it was set between warming house and kitchen in such a way that warmth might be channelled through it. This may be seen at Fountains Abbey, too; in the cold northern air, that warmth was even more important to the community than in the milder air of the south coast.

Hampshire

TITCHFIELD ABBEY (Premonstratensian)

(Off A27, 3 miles west of Fareham)

Like neighbouring Netley Abbey 5 miles to the west, Titchfield also fell into the hands of an ambitious builder who, immediately after the Dissolution, saw its fabric as a desirable asset. Within three years, Thomas Wriothesley had built, as a contemporary writer stated, 'a right stately house embateled and having a goodlye gate, and a conduit in the middle of the court in the very same place where the late Monasterie of Premonstratenses stood, callyd Tichfelde'. In fact, the transformation was even more wholesale than at Netley, though the original layout was ingeniously incorporated in the Tudor edifice, which was given the odd name, 'Place House'.

The key lies in the reference to the 'court'. Though in monasteries of every order the church was the focal point of worship, the *raison d'être* for the existence of the community, the cloister garth was, so to speak, the geographic centre. Round its four sides spread the buildings: usually to the north, the nave of the church; opposite this, the frater and kitchens; on the remaining sides the east and the west ranges enclosing it. But this was also the traditional layout for the larger Tudor dwellings. So, at Titchfield, the cloister garth became the central courtyard; the frater (unusually, to the north of it) became the Great Hall; and the nave was partly demolished to contain an elaborate main entrance with four half-octagonal, two-storey towers built at its corners. The remainder of the nave, to east and west, was used for private apartments. What had been sacred had become, emphatically, secular.

Eighteenth-century engravings show how successfully (from the owner's point of view) this transformation had been effected. By the end of the century, however, much of this had been demolished or had disintegrated, and today the outstanding feature is the fine gatehouse with its lofty and massive towers carved out of (or into) the nave. The visitor can indulge in some leisurely detective-work, sorting out in his mind what lay ready to Wriothesley's hand when he considered a major surgical operation on a property already referred to as 'most naked and barren'. He was fortunate in having the services of a master-mason who had built for Henry VIII the neighbouring castles of Calshot and Hurst.

Herefordshire

DORE ABBEY (Cistercian)

(In Abbey Dore, on B4347, 12 miles south-west of Hereford)

Less is known about the early centuries of this twelfth-century foundation than usual, for in fact all that remains of its conventual buildings is the east end of the church. Almost the whole of the 250ft nave, long ago desecrated by being used to house cattle, has vanished. What you see today is a skilful adaptation of the fabric that survived the Dissolution and was granted to the Scudamore family by Henry VIII. In the first half of the seventeenth century, John Scudamore called on the services of an inspired architect-craftsman, one John Abel, and out of the transepts, crossing, quire and notable east end contrived the lovely church you see today. Incidentally, Dore Abbey church represents the only existing chancel of a Cistercian church in use in England today.

One odd feature that immediately strikes the visitor is the location of the seventeenth-century tower: instead of surmounting the crossing, it is set across the east angle of the south transept. Another odd feature, within the church this time, is the stone slab altar on three squat pillars. It was probably the original high altar; look at it carefully and you will detect slanting gashes in its surface. It was in fact used for generations, first as a dairy cooling-slab and then for meat-salting, before being restored to the church by Viscount Scudamore.

To locate the monastic buildings generally calls for detective work. Grooves high on the north transept wall suggest that a range of buildings ran northwards from it. Certainly cloister and east and west ranges lay to the north instead of to the more usual south of the now-vanished nave. The fact that there is no north window in the north transept confirms this. From here, the sacristy, with the book cupboard in its west wall to serve the monks in the cloister walks, the vestibule to the twelve-sided chapter house, and the distant reredorter, set above the mill stream, extended northwards. Beyond, and well to the east of this, was the infirmary, apparently built actually over the mill stream. There is other evidence—for the expert eye.

Little of all this, however, explicitly confronts you. What is truly beautiful and evocative is the mellow stone church, the work of Scudamore and Abel handling the raw material of the men who built their abbey five centuries before they were born.

Kent

AYLESFORD PRIORY (Carmelite)

(On B2011, 3 miles north-west of Maidstone)

This is still generally known by its ancient name, 'The Friars', and with good reason, for the community that first occupied this site consisted of members of the mendicant order. Their function in life was to go out among those in physical or spiritual need, and minister to them. They had this base, but might be spread widely about the countryside beyond, seeking out those in trouble. They had, in fact, been in trouble themselves. As their name suggests, they originated from Mt Carmel in Palestine, where they had lived as scattered hermits in cells. Unsettled conditions forced them to flee, and one group was sponsored by a crusader, Sir Richard Grey; he was a Kentish landowner, and presented them with his Manor of Aylesford on the Medway. There, in 1242, they were established, and began a new mode of life in a new country.

Like other foundations, including more than thirty other Carmelite houses, they were dissolved. The friars scattered, and their buildings fell into secular hands and remained so for centuries. But the order never abandoned its firm resolve to return, and when, in 1948, the site and buildings were offered for sale, the Prior General of the order appealed for funds to purchase it. Within a year, sufficient had been raised, and the first new community of friars moved in under the leadership of a very remarkable man, Father Malachy Lynch, their first prior.

It was he who, like Abbot Vonier at Buckfast, resolved, under inspiration, to rebuild, re-fashion and enlarge what was suitable among the buildings on the site; and above all, to build and have consecrated a central shrine or sanctuary, dedicated to the Virgin Mary, Mother of God. This, today is the focal point of this great assemblage of chapels and shrines, cloisters, friars' lodgings, chapter house, gatehouse and other buildings. Among these, one of the most interesting is the Pilgrims' Hall which stands practically athwart the ancient Pilgrims' Way by which countless thousands of pious men and women approached the shrine of St Thomas à Becket in Canterbury, 30 miles further to the east. It was a traditional stopping place.

Here ancient and modern meet. Where, seven centuries ago, mendicant friars lived and sought inspiration for their work among the needy, today people of all denominations may forgather and share in the tradition of worship newly revived.

ST AUGUSTINE'S ABBEY (Benedictine)

(In Canterbury)

Not surprisingly, in view of the important part played in England's religious tradition by Canterbury, this late eleventh-century abbey succeeded a number of Anglo-Saxon foundations. The Venerable Bede records that an abbey was founded 'without the city walls' to accommodate monks who came with, and followed, St Augustine from Rome. The year was AD 598. Almost all these very ancient buildings now lie buried beneath the remains that confront you today.

These are of the great abbey which was begun by a monk from Mont St Michel in Normandy (though rather surprisingly named Scotland), who became the first abbot, and on which work was ardently continued under his successor Guido on his death in 1087. Building continued by stages. As at Rievaulx, Tintern and elsewhere, the cloister, frater, kitchen, dorter, chapter house and other appurtenances were laid out on the north, rather than the south side of the church. Unhappily, most of these have long been obliterated or are discernible only to the practised eye. The reason is the usual one—or a variant upon it. At the Dissolution, buildings were demolished on a large scale to provide material for a manor house in the abbey precinct to be used as a posting house for distinguished overseas visitors on their way to pay their respects to Henry VIII, and even, on occasion, for his personal use.

The remains show the church to have become enormous, no less than 349ft in length. Beneath the apsidal presbytery it possessed one of the few truly notable crypts, comparable with those at, for instance, Bury St Edmunds and Gloucester. Beyond the apse are the remains of a later building, a Lady Chapel, completed only just before the Dissolution. Follow this eastwards and you will come upon one of the few really impressive surviving relics of those many pre-Conquest ecclesiastical buildings situated within this huge precinct: the Church (or Chapel) of St Pancras, which dates right back to the era of St Augustine himself.

The broken line of the great north wall of the nave of the abbey church itself leads the eye, over the intervening low roofs, to the soaring majesty of the fifteenth-century Bell Harry Tower of Canterbury Cathedral, known also as Angel Steeple.

Lancashire

CARTMEL PRIORY (Augustinian)

(On B5278, 12 miles east of Ulverston)

The fourteenth-century priory gatehouse, converted into a school in 1642, overlooks the market cross and is the sole survivor of the complex of priory buildings save for the well preserved church hard by. Cartmel Priory Church is among the very few to have survived the Reformation unscathed; at the Dissolution, some of the canons were executed for supporting the Pilgrimage of Grace, but the church was by some means purchased for the parish.

The site on which building began in the late twelfth century was a poor one; the population of the district was sparse and money hard to come by; building often came to a halt until funds became available again. Improvisation became necessary: for example, the cloisters, first laid out on the traditional south side of the nave, had to be moved to the north side. You will find a doorway in the thirteenth-century north transept that led to the canons' dorter. You will note, too, the curious way in which the upper storey of the square tower has been set diagonally on the lower one. There are many other interesting and unusual features at Cartmel that to some extent compensate for the rather cramped appearance of the monastic buildings that survive. The Cromwell Door, for example. This is riddled with bullet-holes, in some of which lead may still be found. They commemorate the anger of the parishioners when Cromwell's soldiers stabled their horses actually within the priory church.

More affluent parishioners have contributed to the church their monumental furnishings during more recent centuries, but it is the medieval that lingers in the memory: the early thirteenth-century work in the so-called Town Quire, with contemporary glass that is worth more than a passing glance. This Town Quire was so named as it was designed for the use of worshipping parishioners rather than the canons themselves. One very unusual feature is the great family pew of the ancient Dicconsons of Wraysholme, fitted with giant casters so that it could be moved about to take advantage of the light and to avoid draughts. Another is the reminder, in the form of a grim tally of burials of men and women overcome by the rising tide while on their way to worship, that until comparatively recently Cartmel could only be approached across the treacherous sands of the bay. At Cartmel, then, it is detail rather than stature that impresses.

Lancashire

FURNESS ABBEY (Cistercian)

(Off A590, 2 miles north of Barrow-in-Furness)

One of the Cistercians' rules laid down that so far as possible their monasteries should be situated 'in places removed from human habitation'. At the time of its founding, and for centuries thereafter, this abbey fulfilled that requirement. The Furness peninsula was difficult of access, save from the north; from the true mainland, the route to it lay over the treacherous Kent Sands of Morecambe Bay. So many people were drowned en route to the abbey that a coroner was appointed, and 'every Christian was stricken with pity'. It is easy enough of access today.

The site certainly conformed to the Cistercian creed of austerity; it lay in a valley that could almost be termed a ravine. So straitened were the precincts that the church had to be orientated north-east to south-west, though not quite so much 'out of true' as Rievaulx Abbey. Another conditioning factor was that of two streams that flowed southwards to east and west. These were vital for drainage purposes. The larger stream flowed southwards from the monks' cemetery to the chapter house, where it divided, one branch flowing beneath the reredorter and thence beneath the guest house and, most ill-advisedly, through the octagonal infirmary kitchen, there to unite with the other watercourse that had served the lay brethren's reredorter before passing beneath the infirmary hall. Modern sanitary inspectors might not wholly approve.

The proximity of the ravine sides was the cause of other curious features. For example, the traditional west tower had to be incorporated in the nave; and for the same reason, most unusually, there is no west door at all. The oldest (early twelfth-century) portion of the church is the south wall of the nave and quire, though the north wall and transepts are not much later. Perhaps the most memorable feature of the abbey as a whole is the chapter house, abutting on the east walk of the cloister garth. Though sadly dilapidated, 'still some trace of majesty forlorn, And a coarse grace remain'. It is noble beauty in disarray; for all the massiveness of its walls, it possesses a curious but compelling element of simplicity that lingers in the memory.

Lancashire

WHALLEY ABBEY (Cistercian)

(On A59, 7 miles north of Blackburn)

This house was founded in the late twelfth century on a site in the Wirral peninsula. Within its first hundred years the site had been flooded so often, its banks so badly eroded, and the buildings so often rendered uninhabitable, that the abbot petitioned the Pope for a new and safer site. His petition was granted, but before the threatened community could organise their move, disaster struck: their church was destroyed by an unprecedented gale, and fire soon afterwards gutted the monastic buildings. Only twenty monks, under Abbot Gregory, escaped from this seemingly doomed site to take up residence at Whalley, on the eastern border of Lancashire, in 1296.

Work proceeded slowly, for stone was not always easy to come by; in fact, it was nearly a hundred years before the church could be consecrated, though the monastic buildings had long been occupied. Then the community began to prosper and was soon in a position to accept guests, distribute food, clothing and footwear to the needy, and even maintain a scholar at Oxford. But any pride thus engendered was severely chastened when, shortly before the Dissolution, the last abbot, John Paslew, was snatched from the abbey for his part in the Pilgrimage of Grace, and summarily hanged.

After the Dissolution the abbey was first neglected and then gradually dismantled to provide building stone for private use; in the seventeenth century the church was almost completely demolished, and with it the monks' dorter and frater. What is to be seen today is a curious mixture of the ancient and the relatively new. The foundations of the church may be recognised by the lines of stone laid out on the turf, and by fragments of its south wall and parts of the south transept; much of the east and west ranges survive, at least in the lower courses of their walls, as does the very unusually shaped octagonal chapter house, for the Cistercians traditionally built these rectangular.

The new, however, has been superimposed upon the old very much more intelligently than was the case in earlier centuries, and certainly with a nobler motive. For now you will find, on the site of Whalley Abbey, a conference house. Established among the noble ruins, it is a focal point in a relatively newly founded centre for religious education: an ancient site, happily brought once more to life in modern terms.

Lincolnshire

CROWLAND ABBEY (Benedictine)

(In Crowland, 10 miles south of Spalding)

This small town lies low on what is called the Bedford Level. Much of this district is so low-lying that its height above sea-level may be measured in feet in single figures. Small wonder, then, that the church tower is a landmark for many miles around in all directions. The whole region has been made familiar to us through the vivid pages of Charles Kingsley's *Hereward the Wake*, and Hereward is said to have been buried in the abbey.

The site is ancient indeed. In the seventh century, St Guthlac, in search of austerity and solitude, drifted hither across the fenlands in a little boat. Certainly he found what he sought in this bleak, windswept, waterlogged stretch of country. He died in 714, and a simple monastery was then built by Ethelwald, King of the Mercians, in fulfilment of a vow. It was soon laid waste by the Danes but in the twelfth century a new monastery was founded on the hallowed site and building proceeded throughout that and the following centuries, to the greater glory of God and St Guthlac.

All too little of the abbey remains today, but enough to hint at its splendour. Though quire and presbytery, transepts and crossing tower and other buildings were successively razed to the ground, save for isolated lengths of wall and the bases of some buttresses, the nave was so huge that its north aisle alone constitutes the parish church today. You approach it along East Street, to be confronted by the beautiful west end which is dominated above by its squat tower and louvred steeple and on its south side by the remains of what was the original west entrance, a noble ghost, hollow-eyed but memorable. Sculptures beside and above the huge window depict scenes from St Guthlac's life.

Look up as you enter by the north aisle porch, now the main entrance. Above you is a 'parvise', or priest's room, now a small chapel; it is a comparatively rare feature among surviving abbeys and priories today. Look eastwards: a sequence of piers and plinths and broken columns reveals something of the stature of this great church as it was seven centuries ago, though so much of it has long since vanished. But the ancient church is alive still, for Crowland folk and others now worship where once the Benedictines, monks and lay-brethren alike, bowed in prayer and praise.

THORNTON ABBEY (Augustinian)

(Off A160, 4 miles south-east of Barton on Humber)

Founded as a House of Canons Regular of St Augustine (the 'Black Canons') in the twelfth century by twelve monks from Kirkham Priory, it occupies a desolate site on low-lying ground washed by the Humber. Only the dorter survives of the twelfth-century building; the remainder is almost all of thirteenth- and fourteenth-century date.

Strangely, the immediate impression is of a castle rather than an abbey. Its most striking feature is the magnificent gatehouse, which ranks among the finest in England. It served as the abbot's lodging—and lodging on a magnificent scale. The crenellated tops of its four octagonal towers rise to nearly 50ft. A seventeenth-century writer, Abraham de la Pryme, recorded that there were 'upon every exalted turret and stone of the battlements, men with swords, shields, poll-axes etc in their hands, looking downwards. The battlements seemed to be covered with armed men'. Those figures, surely most inappropriate for an abbey, have long vanished; to know what they looked like you must visit the forbidding gatehouse of Alnwick Castle, where similar giant and terrifying figures still dominate the walls. But the portcullis grooves may still be seen at Thornton Abbey, and its precinct is still partly encircled by a dry moat.

Unquestionably, however, the most beautiful (as opposed to striking) relic of the abbey today is that of the chapter house. Built as an octagon, three of its walls yet survive, standing to the apex of their soaring windows. The window-tracery is of trefoil, quatrefoil and cinquefoil, and in a marvellous state of preservation.

Here at Thornton, the purist may spend his time establishing the points at which one century's masonry replaced that of another and earlier one. The romantically inclined will be tempted to look for what remains of 'the little hollow room'; it is to be found between the north-west wall of the chapter house and the parlour. It was, almost certainly, the abbey's strong-room. But here, if legend is to be believed (and why should it not?) some centuries ago one of the Black Canons was found, walled up. He was seated at a table, pen in hand, an open book in front of him. On the opening of his living tomb he disintegrated into dust, like some Egyptian mummy too suddenly exposed to the rush of fresh air.

Monmouthshire

LLANTHONY PRIORY (Augustinian)

(On B4423, 8 miles north of Abergavenny)

The story of how this twelfth-century priory came into being is a more 'human' one than is usual in these accounts, whatever the monastic order concerned may have been; indeed, it has something of the quality of a fable, or biblical parable, about it. A knight out hunting in the Honddu Valley took shelter from a sudden storm in a ruined chapel dedicated to the patron saint of Wales, David. There, like Saul some twelve centuries earlier, he suddenly 'saw the light', and was instantly converted. He proceeded to gather about him a chaplain and a few like-minded pious men and, with the subsequent patronage of Henry I and Matilda, established this very early priory.

Like Benedictine Lindisfarne (and others), it flourished, was raped and abandoned and flourished again until, at the Dissolution, it ceased to exist as a priory. But it was not entirely neglected. It became a royal grace-and-favour abode; in the eighteenth century a Colonel Wood utilised the south tower (incredibly) as a shooting-box and established his steward in the priory; in the early nineteenth century the writer W. S. Landor acquired it and set up in style as a country gentleman for a few unhappy years. And today, the whole of the surviving west range (traditionally designed for the lay brethren) has become a licensed guest-house, one of the vaulted basements actually being fitted out as a bar.

Still, the two massive west towers and the shell of the crossing tower between the fine transepts, with the presbytery, sufficiently dominate the whole to enable one to ignore this relatively modern conversion to secular use—which, in spite of its convenience, will surely be deplored by most sensitive visitors to this lovely priory in its broad valley site. They will rejoice to find that the little slype, between chapter house and south transept, is no longer a garage and now clearly reveals its ancient function as passageway and inner and very secluded parlour. The cloister, too, is interesting in that, most unusually, it does not constitute an exact square.

Perhaps because of the inescapable awareness of the descent from the sublime to the utilitarian, it is best to contemplate this priory from a slight distance: the undoubted best viewpoint is from the level pastureland immediately to the north of it.

Monmouthshire

TINTERN ABBEY (Cistercian)

(Off A466, 5 miles north of Chepstow)

The visitor will agree that Tintern occupies a site as beautiful as its melodious name implies: on the right bank of the Wye, 6 miles above its union with the Severn. The river is here enclosed between steep slopes, with a rocky crest immediately above its left bank; immediately behind the abbey the ground slopes only less steeply away from it to the south, thickly tree clad. To the monks who arrived there in 1131 it may have seemed somewhat forbidding, and more deserving than Rievaulx was of the comment by an early monk chronicler to the effect that that site was 'a place of horror and waste solitude'.

The site presented one problem. Traditionally, the general monastic buildings, including the cloister, infirmary, abbot's lodging, fraters and dorters, kitchens and store rooms, were always laid out on the south side of the church. But on this site, problems of drainage, among others, entailed building these ancillaries on the north side, nearest to the river. The church, as usual, was of course orientated east-west, parallel with the river; there was not, here, the same problem as at Rievaulx.

What you find at Tintern is almost all thirteenth- and early fourteenth-century work, though there was an earlier church. The abbey church, apart from a collapsed roof, stands almost entire: a superb edifice soaring into the heavens from the level sward all about it and reflected in the waters close by. An interesting feature of the cloister may be seen in the remains of the canopied seat, on the south walk, used by the prior whose duty it was to superintend the monks during their meditations.

Another and very unusual feature here is the 'barrow-way': a low arch at the east end of the presbytery through which building materials were brought in from outside. Yet another unusual feature is to be found in the warming house. Its original hearth was centrally placed on four piers, and so designed that it could radiate warmth all round. This, as always, was the only hearth available to the monks, apart from the fires in kitchen and infirmary. As for the water supply, it did not come from the river flowing below and to the north of the abbey but was piped from a spring in the hillside to the south, appropriately named Coldwell. There is a serenity about this river site that is hardly surpassed anywhere else in the country.

Norfolk

CASTLE ACRE PRIORY (Cluniac)

(Off A1065, 4 miles north of Swaffham)

This immensely ancient religious house, much of its fabric dating from the second half of the eleventh century, was founded by William de Warenne who came to England with William the Conqueror, or by his son, also William. He generously endowed it, and there is originality in the form his endowment took, for it included not only 15 acres of land, five shillings rent of land, and one garden, but 'two thousand eels from Methwold' (a village some miles to the south noted for these). Hardly less important, he handed over a serf named Ulmar who already had some repute as a worker in the local stone and flint, and threw in the serf's well-worked garden for good measure.

The priory's mother-church was in far away Cluny in Burgundy, and this led to continual trouble over the contributions demanded by the religious house in France. There were signs of revolt, and discipline became lax. Within two centuries, Edward III had to send his serjeant-at-arms to round up certain of the Castle Acre monks who had 'spurned the habit of their Order and were become vagabonds in secular habit'. They were duly delivered to the prior for fitting (and probably harsh) chastisement.

Looking today at this peaceful scene on the sloping north bank of the little Nar, you would not think that it could ever have been the setting for a disciplinary visit from a monarch's serjeant-at-arms. It sleeps where it stands, on the western fringe of a sleeping village. The west front is an outstanding example of twelfth-century design and craftsmanship; its south tower still stands four storeys in height, though unhappily the nave walls are much dilapidated. Abutting on to the south tower is the prior's lodging, in which good use has been made of the local building material, Norfolk flint. The discerning eye will distinguish here between the twelfth-century work and that superimposed upon it, notably the beautiful corbelled window.

The cloister garth is a perfect square with sides 100ft in length, and to the east, the chapter house, monks' dorter and reredorter still stand to the height of their upper windows. An interesting feature of this last (apart from its two upstanding gables) is the fact that, built on a lower slope, towards the Nar, its upper floor was connected with the adjacent dorter by a bridge.

Norfolk

THETFORD PRIORY (Cluniac)

(In Thetford)

Like Castle Acre Priory, this was founded by one of William the Conqueror's closest associates. Not William de Warenne, however, but the old soldier, Roger Bigod. He himself laid the foundation stone (and died a week afterwards). Real fame did not come to the priory until a century later when what might be termed a miracle focussed the attention of the religious-minded everywhere.

A local artisan, suffering from an incurable disease, prayed to Our Lady of Thetford to be cured. She appeared to him in a vision and told him to order the prior to build her a Lady Chapel. The prior, foolishly, and to save money, built one of wood. She then bade a woman of Thetford to tell the prior that the chapel must be of stone. Foolishly, the woman ignored the order and was immediately struck down with paralysis. The prior heard of this, repented, and built the Lady Chapel of fine stone. He placed above the altar an image of Our Lady, and it was found that there was a hollow in her head, part-filled with holy relics. The story does not say whether either the artisan or the woman recovered; and it does indeed seem unfair that the obstinate prior should have got away with it unscathed. Indeed, he was the one to profit, for word got about and the priory soon became wealthy as a result of the pilgrimages made to it by hordes of sick men and women in the sure hope of being healed of their ills.

Part of the Lady Chapel still stands to almost its original height. An interesting feature is the remains of a spiral stair in the north-west corner which led to the small 'watching-room' occupied by the monk on duty during these pilgrimages. There is still much twelfth-century work to be seen, as well as that of the next century. The south wall of the twelfth-century quire still rises to a considerable height, as does the south wall of the frater. And here is an interesting detail: in the fourteenth century, three buttresses were built to brace this wall. They have now subsided and detached themselves, but the wall they were built to reinforce stands as firm as ever.

Finally, the gatehouse has survived and is indeed one of the priory's most impressive (though not most ancient) remains. Look for the fine knapped-flint work on walls that still rise to three storeys in height.

Norfolk

WALSINGHAM PRIORY (Augustinian)

(In Little Walsingham, on B1105, 5 miles north of Fakenham)

'O little town of Walsingham, How still we see thee lie!' The substitution for 'Bethlehem' in this line from the well-known hymn is easily justified, for this whole region has been known since medieval times as England's Holy Land. From its intimate association with the Virgin Mary, whose shrine in 'The Holy House of Walsingham' has been here since her miraculous appearance in 1051, the little town has repeatedly been referred to both as Nazareth and as Bethlehem. Founded about 1150, the priory soon became an object of pilgrimage from all over Christendom. Every English monarch from Henry III onwards came here as a pilgrim; often they left their footgear at the so-called Slipper Chapel a mile from the shrine, and completed the pilgrimage barefoot like the humbler pilgrims. Henry VIII himself came in 1511 and kept a candle burning at the shrine until, ironically, he dissolved the priory along with all the others.

For years it lapsed as a centre of pilgrimage but the tradition was revived at about the turn of last century, though today there is much less to see here than was known to medieval pilgrims. There is the very impressive east wall of the church, with a huge window and two turrets, and though once there was a crossing tower balanced by a west tower (as at Wymondham today), no more than a hint of these features now survives. But the south wall of the frater, a good example of early thirteenth-century work, is largely intact and still contains the stairs that led to the pulpitum. At its entrance from the south-west corner of the original cloisters you can still see the remains of the lavatorium.

The west range has largely vanished, but in the east range several bays of the undercroft that supported the dorter are still to be seen. The gatehouse that gave entry to the precinct, however, still stands. Less spectacular than, say, the one at Battle or St Osyth's, it nevertheless beautifully matches the ambience of this gracious little town where so many buildings are memorable. Pass through it, continue by way of the splendid Norman arch beyond the east end of the church that towers above the trees, and you will come upon the twin wells that almost certainly date from before the Conquest and have always been credited with possessing restorative properties, because of their proximity to the shrine of the Blessed Virgin Mary, Our Lady of Walsingham.

Norfolk

WYMONDHAM ABBEY (Benedictine)

(On A11, 9 miles south-west of Norwich)

The Abbey Church of St Mary and St Thomas of Canterbury, still in use after nearly nine centuries, strikes the observer as somewhat odd when viewed across the so-called Abbey Meadows, for it possesses two strongly differentiated towers, one at either end. In fact, these represent a 'story in stone', for they are the monumental record of an unusual and prolonged unhappy relationship between the monks and the people whom the church was designed jointly to serve.

Built on the site of a Saxon chapel, the priory was founded in 1107, and for the succeeding three centuries and more, twenty-seven priors ruled here; in the mid-fifteenth century the priory was elevated to the status of an abbey, and ten abbots held sway here until the Dissolution. It is clear from the records that throughout many of those centuries there was dissension here that culminated in outbreaks of strife and even violence between the monks and the growing numbers of parishioners. The church had been noted for the magnificence of its unbroken view from west to east. Resenting the parishioners' rights, the monks built a wall, to ceiling height, to shut them out; it was a brutal line of demarcation in the days before this had become a vogue phrase. The parishioners reacted by invading the priory, seizing the prior and locking him up throughout the important Feast of Epiphany. The monks, on a dubious pretext, dismantled the original tower, transferred the bells, and began to build another. The parishioners this time reacted by declaring that they could no longer hear the summons to worship, and petitioned the highest authority for a permit to construct a bell tower of their own. The permit was received, and the result is the imposing, if somewhat stark west tower, in Perpendicular style, that dominates the west end of the nave to this day. Its date is mid-fifteenth century: evidence that the conflict had already been sustained for all too long a period of time.

The older tower, of course, is the beautiful octagonal one, built by the monks two centuries before to replace the original lantern tower. Almost the only reminder of the priory as it originally was is the noble arch of the now vanished chapter house to be seen on the south side of the church, beneath the memorable octagonal tower that graces the eastern end. One accepts its beauty, and forgets the background.

BLANCHLAND ABBEY (Premonstratensian)

(On B6306, 8 miles south of Hexham)

There is probably no stranger relic of an abbey or priory than this in all England; and probably no surviving religious house of which there is less to be seen while what survives is of such interest. For Blanchland (the village) *is* Blanchland Abbey —the abbey of the *blanc,* or 'White', Canons, as this order was often called. What makes it unique is the fact that the entire village that you see today is built out of the material, and on the foundations, of an abbey established in this 'lost' corner of our northernmost county in 1159.

Enter its Outer Precinct, or L-shaped Second Courtyard, by way of the ancient gatehouse and, immediately on your left, is the Lord Crewe Arms. This was actually the abbot's lodging, on the west side of the cloister; adjoining it was the guests' lodging; adjoining this, the kitchen. Its great fireplace is still to be seen in what is now a hotel bearing the name of the man who, in the eighteenth century, built Blanchland as we see it today. Abutting on to this was the monks' frater, at right angles to it and occupying, as usual, the south side of the cloister. It is now an elegant row of cottages, built, like the rest of Blanchland, of the abbey stone.

There is another row of stone-built cottages at right angles to this, following what was the line of the monks' dorter seven centuries ago. The buildings continuing northwards from the end of this row would have been the abbey parlour, the chapter house and the south transept—now, alas, no more. What you can see today of the church is no more than the quire, the north transept and a tower beyond this; in fact, it is not the original church but one built by the canons a century after they took up residence. The cloister, according to custom, was laid out on the south side of the now-vanished nave; today it is represented by the lawn and walks immediately behind the Lord Crewe Arms.

Over the years, legends have proliferated. One of them accounts for the material dissolution of the abbey thus: her pealing bells were heard by a party of Scottish raiders hopelessly lost in mist on the fells of this wild borderland. They were guided by them to safety—and an unexpected prize. Showing base ingratitude, they sacked the abbey and slaughtered its occupants. It is hard, in a place so serene, to accept so improbable a story as that.

Northumberland (Holy Island)

LINDISFARNE PRIORY (Benedictine)

(Off the coast, 3 miles from Beal)

Seven centuries ago the Isle of Lindisfarne was given to Aidan, the missionary bishop, as the site for a monastery. A century later, it was to be the bridge-head by which the first Danes invaded Britain; it was the first victim of their savagery. Intermittently, Aidan's followers rebuilt their monastery, fled from further onslaughts (or were massacred to a man), returned to their island, and fled once more. It was impossible to establish a monastery in that tortured island until the eleventh century. Then a group of Benedictine monks from Durham moved in. They found no remains whatsoever of any buildings erected by their predecessors, so they set about building the priory whose remains confront the visitor today. As a gesture towards the future they re-named Lindisfarne 'Holy Island'. The name appears on the atlas today but the priory itself is still Lindisfarne, the ancient name.

The island remained vulnerable, the monastery permanently at risk. Partially protected by a basalt ridge to the south, it was also in part fortified. The keen eye will detect a pair of crossbow-loops beneath the ruined gable of the west front of the church—a tell-tale feature that emphasises its vulnerability. There was a small fort, too; but nothing of that remains today.

A lonely site indeed. It is accessible only at low tide, when the long causeway is temporarily laid bare. Not surprisingly, it was never a flourishing religious house like, for instance, Fountains Abbey. Amenities for the monks were restricted. There was not the traditional covered walk round the cloister garth in which they could walk, meditate and read while sheltered from wind and rain. But they did have (and must, on that bleak, wind-swept island site, have gratefully welcomed) the traditional warming room, the open fireplace and chimney of which may be seen to this day, and must surely be ghost-surrounded by night. The church, with its six-bay nave, completed early in the twelfth century and flanked by two small transepts, is impressive; the west wall of the north transept still stands almost to its original height.

Certainly the dominant impression made by Lindisfarne Priory is that of its extreme isolation and hence the bleakness of the life led by its small, dedicated community of monks subsisting under the authority of a succession of lonely priors.

Northumberland

TYNEMOUTH PRIORY (Benedictine)

(At Tynemouth, 9 miles north-east of Newcastle)

The north bank of the Tyne, at its outlet in the North Sea, rises to an impressive headland whose cliffs fall steeply on three sides; not surprisingly, this has been a fortified site ever since Roman times almost to the present day. A succession of strong-points and monastic cells left relics beneath the turf, but it was not until the late eleventh century that the first stones of the priory to be seen today were laid. Of these, most constitute the main walls of the nave, one wall of the monks' dorter and warming house and, curiously enough, their reredorter. The promontory still carries castle as well as priory; down the ages they have been closely associated, under ever-changing conditions of war and peace.

The entire site is dominated by the awe-inspiring walls of the presbytery, which still, after nearly eight centuries, rise to more than 70ft—almost their original height. No doubt conscious of the power of the prevailing north-easterly gales, the builders took no chances: these walls are more than 7ft thick, and the vaulting is still intact to a height of more than 50ft. Standing detached from the now-vanished quire, this giant structure has an overwhelming dignity; it is somehow reminiscent (though architecturally so different) of, say, the remains of the Temple of Apollo at Corinth.

The west end of the nave is early thirteenth-century work. It does not compare in height with the east end, but it contains a very remarkable doorway, of enormous depth, in which no fewer than five successive moulded orders carry the eye inwards one behind the other. At the extreme far end, beyond the lofty walls of the presbytery, is the most interesting single building, a chapel added to the church in the middle of the fifteenth century. The interior rather than the exterior commands interest and survives uppermost in the memory. Note the superb vaulting, the thirty-three fine bosses at the intersections of the stone ribs, and, not least important, the seated figure of St Osin, a hermit who lived in pain and died in humility alone on this site in the chill winter of 1126. Kneeling at the saint's feet is the priory's founder, Robert de Mowbray, Earl of Northumberland—hence the name of the chantry, the Percy Chantry, Percy being the name of the great Northumberland clan that dominated the Border country for so many generations.

Shropshire

BUILDWAS ABBEY (Cistercian)

(On B4380, 4 miles north of Much Wenlock)

Known originally as the Abbey of Our Lady and St Chad, this is a daughter-house of Furness Abbey, in Lancashire, though it was founded in 1135 by the Bishop of Coventry and Lichfield. It occupies a beautiful site, on low-lying ground between the north-eastern tip of Wenlock Edge and the great mass that is topped by The Wrekin at 1,385ft. Unfortunately it is sufficiently near to the Welsh Marches to have suffered from time to time from what contemporary chroniclers referred to as the 'levity of the Welsh'. Details make it clear that this was not mere 'light-heartedness'; on the contrary, the word had a more sinister connotation. In 1350 the Abbot of Buildwas suffered the indignity of being snatched from his lodging and imprisoned by a gang of marauders from across the border. Some years later, Owen Glendower's men ravaged the estates from which the abbey drew its sole revenue. Attack even came from within the precinct. There is a record of a renegade monk, Thomas Tonge, who murdered his abbot. He escaped, and actually had the effrontery in due course to petition to be readmitted to the order he had so criminally disgraced.

Because the site slopes fairly steeply to the north and west, the cloister and other buildings had to be laid out, contrary to custom, on the north side of the church. Work proceeded apace, and it is known that by the end of the twelfth century the abbey buildings were completed. Much of the church itself still stands, notably the presbytery and north and south transepts, in each of which two small chapels were built into the east walls. Perhaps because of the slope of the ground, there was no doorway in the west end, though the west front is still in good condition. Nor was there a tower to flank the west front; but a tower was built over the crossing, and may be seen to this day.

The slope northwards probably accounts also for the relatively sparse remains of the north range, that would have been laid out between the west and east ranges. Beyond the chapter house and parlour to the east, and the lay-brothers' range to the west, there is little to be seen. A fragment of the monks' dorter; even less of their frater; no sign (as yet) of kitchen or warming house or infirmary. But excavation still to be undertaken may well reveal these essential monastic buildings at Buildwas.

Shropshire

LILLESHALL ABBEY (Augustinian)

(Off A518, 3 miles south of Newport)

Like the Cistercians, the Augustinians chose as far as possible to site their houses in isolated spots. This one, however, is much less remote than most; the Cluniac priory of Wenlock is not 12 miles distant, and Cistercian Buildwas Abbey is nearer still. Founded in 1148 by Richard de Belmeis, Lilleshall rapidly became one of the more important houses of its order. Successive abbots were granted special rights, which included permission to hunt over the countryside adjoining one of the royal forests. Within a century of its foundation, Henry III himself had stayed as a guest on more than one occasion while hunting in the locality.

More of the abbey would survive today had it not been for the fact that, as at St Botolph's, Colchester, it became embroiled in the Civil War. Another Richard, Richard Leveson, turned the abbey into a royalist strongpoint; it withstood a siege of several weeks, until finally and disastrously entry was effected through the north transept. Three centuries later it suffered from a more unusual attack: coal-mining activities extended beneath the precinct and as a result portions of the surviving buildings began to subside. The finest part of the church, its eastern end, had to be put into a strait-jacket and substantially reinforced in case it should collapse.

Happily, this end of the church, together with much of the east range, including sacristy and chapter house, and the frater which constitutes the whole of the south range, still stands to a very fair height. The body of the nave has lasted less well, but the tower flanking the beautiful west doorway is outstandingly fine even though severely truncated. There is another door, that leading from the north-east corner of the cloister into the crossing and quire, which is a truly remarkable specimen of elaborate Romanesque work in what is perhaps an unexpected setting. And near by, too, is possibly the most remarkable of all surviving examples of the traditional book-locker or cupboard, replenished from the library behind it and used by the monks at meditation. Its ornamental tympanum above the twin compartments shows that it was designed with love as well as with mere masons' skill. All the masonry, incidentally, is of the mellow red or russet sandstone characteristic of the region, one which adds warmth and intimacy to what in any case is ancient and therefore memorable.

Shropshire

WENLOCK PRIORY (Cluniac)

(At Much Wenlock, 12 miles south-east of Shrewsbury)

Located at the north-eastern end of lovely Wenlock Edge, for ever associated with A. E. Housman, this is one of the very few surviving Cluniac foundations in England. It has a strange, even haunting, history. Largely built in the thirteenth century (though the fine chapter house is twelfth-century work), it is on an ancient, hallowed site. In the seventh century there was a nunnery here whose abbess was Milburge, daughter of the King of Mercia. After her death in AD 722 she was canonised, and a tradition of miraculous happenings began and lasted until the Dissolution.

One tradition holds that her bones were found in a silver casket by monks digging on the site at the inspired bidding of the Archbishop of Canterbury. Another, more picturesque, states that a small boy fell into a cavity when the floor of the priory was being laid, and revealed a coffin containing her bones. Certainly she was always associated with miracles. Only half a century before the Dissolution it became necessary to repair the vaulted roof over quire and altar. Skilled workmen were called in by Prior Richard, and the more able monks deputed to assist them. The whole of the roof had to be dismantled, inside the east end of the church. This involved long ladders, scaffolding, pulleys and ropes. There were grave accidents: ladders collapsed, scaffolding disintegrated, ropes broke. One after another, artisans and monks fell from the vaulted roof to the stone paving of the church. They fell from a great height yet not one of them sustained more than minor injuries, and each one of them recovered instantly and completely in the priory infirmary. There was no question but that St Milburge was watching over those who strove to improve and beautify the church built on the site of her ancient nunnery.

All too little, however, survives today. There is exceptionally beautiful wall ornamentation on the south side of the chapter house; the church impresses with its sense of timelessness and peace; there are the remains of an interesting octagonal lavatorium in the cloister garth; one great gable soars into the heavens from the end of the south transept. The site is hardly less lovely today than it was when King Merewald's daughter became abbess of the nunnery there nearly thirteen hundred years ago.

Somerset

CLEEVE ABBEY (Cistercian)

(At Washford, 4 miles south-east of Dunster)

Perhaps because so little of the actual church has survived, Cleeve is all too often overlooked by those who are interested in the religious houses of England. A pity, this, because Cleeve is in fact probably the best example of the layout of an abbey to be found anywhere in the country. The church may be little more than the ghost of its former self, for little survives other than its south wall and parts of the presbytery and south transept; but many of the basic features of a monastery are to be seen here at their best, notably the great east and south ranges. Even though much of the former is early thirteenth century, it is in an exceptionally fine state of preservation.

Traditionally, this range includes the monks' dorter and reredorter, chapter house and library, sacristy, parlour and slype. Over these last, at Cleeve, rides the magnificent dorter, a dormitory 137ft long and 25ft broad. True, its roof is of later date; but connoisseurs rate the dorter, built in the thirteenth century, among the finest in existence, and perhaps the very finest of all.

Many of the chambers are not only well preserved but retain the decoration given to them seven centuries ago. In the sacristy, for instance, there is some fine plasterwork. Below the south range there is a beautiful tiled floor, that of the first frater, replaced by one at right angles to it to conform to Cistercian practice. In the later one, you can still see the base of the pulpitum from which the reading-monk read aloud to his brethren at table. The north wall of the cloister (the south wall of the nave) contains a hint of the 'Collation Seat' occupied by the abbot when he read from the *Collationes Patrum* before the service of Compline.

There is, too, a more unusual relic. In the south-east corner of the reredorter, on the upper floor, the wall is pierced by a diagonal 'squint'. It was designed to house a lantern so placed that it could light both dorter and reredorter at the same time; the iron ring from which the lantern was hung is still in place, a trivial but somehow revealing feature of monastic life. And there is much more besides. Here at Cleeve, too often neglected, you will find better than almost anywhere else in the country, a clear picture-in-depth of monastic life in its heyday prior to the Dissolution.

Somerset

GLASTONBURY ABBEY (Benedictine)

(In Glastonbury)

This is, without question, the oldest religious foundation in the country. There was a Christian church here when Britain was a Roman province; it survived as a sanctuary into Saxon times; churches came and went, but the site remained a sacred one and is sacred to this day. In view of its antiquity it has amassed a greater corpus of legend than any other religious site. It is said that twelve disciples of the Apostle Philip settled here thirty years after Christ's death and, at the express bidding of the Archangel Gabriel, built a little chapel of wattle-and-daub. Here, Joseph of Arimathea is said to have planted the Holy Thorn, alleged to blossom once a year at Christmastide; here, too, he is said to have secreted the Holy Grail containing drops of Christ's blood. And here too, if persistent tradition is not to be flouted, lies the body of King Arthur: Glastonbury and Avalon are inextricably interwoven in legend.

The earliest buildings were destroyed by the Danes. St Dunstan became abbot of the rebuilt abbey in the mid-tenth century; two centuries later fire obliterated the abbey, and what you see today dates from the late twelfth century, the thirteenth and fourteenth. Among the oldest portions is the shell of St Mary's Chapel. Several bays of the south aisle wall, the great piers of the crossing and fragments of the north transept and chancel survived the depredations of Cromwell and later vandals, and the outlines of this abbey church laid out in stone on the velvet turf show it to have been nearly 600ft long and 90ft in width—larger than any church in England today.

One of these medieval buildings still stands virtually intact: the near-unique Abbot's Kitchen, octagonal in design and culminating in a beautiful central louvre resembling a church lantern in miniature, to which the smoke from the corner fireplace was carried by a system of flues. It stands apart from the surviving monastic buildings such as the dortors, frater and abbot's quarters which would have been associated with it. Practically all of these have long since vanished from this spacious greensward site, dominated from afar by Glastonbury Tor on which the last of the abbots was criminally executed for alleged treason in November 1539, by the ruthless and grasping Henry VIII.

Suffolk

BURY ST EDMUNDS ABBEY (Benedictine)

The noblest remains of this abbey—in its heyday a rival in power to Glastonbury itself—are the two gatehouses. They give access to a precinct that once covered 16 acres and contained a church (the third to be built on the site) no less than 500ft long. Its fame largely derived from the fact that the martyred King Edmund's body was buried there. Alleged to work miracles, it became an object of pilgrimages in which even monarchs took part. At the shrine, the barons swore to make a king yield to their will—and Magna Carta was the result.

Little remains today of the ancient monastic buildings which, after vicissitudes, fell victim to the Dissolution. Two arches from the eleventh-century church have been incorporated in the fabric of some relatively modern buildings, and there are signs of the kitchen and dorter walls here and there, as mounds beneath the turf. Dove House represents a tower that once stood proudly. There are the remains of a flint-built chapel, though this no longer serves its original purpose in the precinct. A few isolated columns, ghosts of their former selves, still stand, much truncated, often in private gardens adjoining. But the two great gatehouses are there still.

The Abbey Gateway, in Decorated style of the fourteenth century, with canopied niches, traceried panels, slender clustered shafts and a shield bearing the arms of Edward the Confessor, rises to 60ft and more and welcomes you into the precinct from Angel Hill. Not far away is the 86ft high, massive, square, uncompromising Norman tower, older by centuries, and claiming with good reason to be among the finest such towers in the country. It was once the gateway to the abbey graveyard but today it is no museum piece, for it now houses the bells of St James's Church, Bury St Edmunds' cathedral.

The precinct into which the two towers were designed to give access remains among England's more hallowed sites for St Edmund is still remembered, and some believe that even today, as in former times, miracles are wrought in his name. It is strange, however, that no antiquarian has come forward to prove (or disprove) the fond belief that the bones of the martyred king still lie where they were brought for burial so many centuries ago, in the township that bears his hallowed name.

BATTLE ABBEY (Benedictine)

(In Battle)

Unless the very name aroused an echo in your memory, you might not suspect that this quiet township lies on the edge of England's most historic battlefield—none other than that of '1066 And All That'. A feature, however, at the south end of the main street will confirm the echo: the magnificent battlemented gatehouse through which you may pass to the site of the Battle of Hastings itself. What you will find, however, does not resemble a battlefield; nor will you find much of the abbey to which the fourteenth-century gatehouse gave access.

The abbey built here some 900 years ago was established on the direct orders of William the Conqueror himself, at the suggestion of an associate, a monk from Marmoutier. He made a huge grant of recently-conquered land—with a radius of a mile and a half from the focal point, which was to be the high altar of the abbey yet to be built, set (so tradition holds) on the exact spot of the battlefield where King Harold was slain. He made himself responsible for the whole cost of building, and stipulated that it should be of stone from the quarries of Caen in his native Normandy.

Enter today by the central arch of this noble gatehouse, and what confronts you? The abbey church has vanished, though the foundations of the five chapels at the east end of the presbytery may still be seen. A fine range of buildings on the east side of the vanished cloister once included the monks' dorter with their common house below it and a further building that probably housed the novices. Facing this, on the west side of the cloister, were the abbot's lodging and the parlour, first built in the thirteenth century and later restored. In the south-west corner of the precinct there are two tall octagonal towers marking the western end of the once-splendid Princess Elizabeth's Lodging, designed, after the Dissolution, by Henry VIII's Master of Horse, Sir Anthony Browne, to accommodate the girl who was to become Elizabeth I. It was erected on the sub-vault of the abbey's chief guesthouse, a building nearly 200ft in length. It is empty today, but the abbot's lodging and other adjacent buildings are now occupied, fittingly or otherwise, by a girls' school, at least as temporary residents. It may truly be said that they have history all about them, and beneath their very feet.

MICHELHAM PRIORY (Augustinian)

(On B2108, 8 miles north-west of Eastbourne)

On an island site, surrounded by a wide moat fed from the River Cuckmere, lie the remains of a priory founded in 1229 by Gilbert de Laigle, a Norman lord who was a great landowner. The site he chose already had a moat dug by earlier Normans when they took over an earlier Saxon settlement in the wide valley. A prior and twelve canons, symbolising Christ and His twelve apostles, went into residence. This number remained constant until the priory was decimated by the Black Death in 1349. It never fully recovered; indeed, it seemed to lose heart. Later in the century it was threatened by the Peasants' Revolt, and this led to the building of the fortified gatehouse and tower, through which to this day you must enter the precinct.

Trouble of a different kind followed. Discipline became lax and there were punitive visitations from the bishop. With the degeneration of the moral tone (canons had been caught frequenting local taverns!) the buildings also fell into disrepair. By the Dissolution they were already decaying, and afterwards material was stolen and the moat began to silt up.

Happily, in the late sixteenth century one Herbert Pelham built himself a Tudor mansion at the south end of the west range. It still stands there, entered by way of the stone-vaulted parlour and buttery with the thirteenth-century prior's room over it. The site then passed into the hands of the Buckhurst family, and for nearly three hundred years such buildings as remained were cherished and rehabilitated. Though nothing remains of the priory church, its outline has been recorded with white stone set in the velvet turf, its High Altar by a cluster of evergreen shrubs—a symbolic touch.

Herbert Pelham's fine Tudor wing at the south end of the west range is intact, and intelligently filled with contemporary furniture and fittings. His Tudor kitchen separates it from what remains of the canons' refectory, the older and the more recent masonry being successfully 'married' one to the other. In a corner of the refectory you can see the narrow stone stairway leading to the pulpitum from which the scriptures were daily read to the canons at table. Here, especially, the thirteenth-century work and the sixteenth-century work call for appreciation. All about the remains of these buildings are lawns, flower beds and noble trees, with the glint of water from moat and pond to enliven the scene.

Westmorland

SHAP ABBEY (Premonstratensian)

(Off A6, 10 miles south of Penrith)

As usual with this order, the site selected was remote, inconvenient, isolated. It is a very cramped site, too: a narrow valley through which flows the River Lowther, skirting the abbey precinct on its eastern side. So cramped is it that the presbytery is almost on the left bank of the river. High hills surround the site on all sides.

As so often, one structure dominates the whole site. Here it is the great west tower, built in 1500 after it had been found impossible to build it over the crossing between the transepts. The ground was more stable at the west end, and the tower still stands almost to its original height, its walls 7ft thick at the base, and strengthened by beautifully graduated angle buttresses. From the exterior it presents a somewhat gaunt, craggy appearance; within its containing walls, however, you will find that much of the pavement of smallish, square flagstones is still as it was when the monks and lay brethren processed through its great arch.

By contrast, the nave is sadly diminished. It was built during two different periods of the thirteenth century and the practised eye may be able to distinguish between them; as usual, the western end was built later than the eastern end, for presbytery and quire took precedence over the rest. A very unusual feature of this ruined nave, however (paralleled, incidentally, at Easby), is to be found in a series of part-circles deep-incised into the stone floor of the nave just short of the arch separating it from the quire. These marked the exact positions to be taken up by the canons at the close of their ritual Sunday processing through the monastic buildings to the focal point of their abbey church.

Another interesting and rare feature is explained by a generous gesture from the 7th Earl of Lonsdale. He recently returned to the abbey a number of worked stones that had been removed from it at the Dissolution and incorporated in his ancestors' Lowther Castle. They have now been replaced, in the nave and in the chapter house, as the bases of pillars. And one more feature: a leper-squint in a corner of the quire, aligned on the altar. There was a leper hospital at Appleby, 7 miles distant, that was under the jurisdiction of Shap Abbey. Was this squint incorporated for the benefit of these unhappy persons, isolated far from the valley-site?

Wiltshire

MALMESBURY ABBEY (Benedictine)

(In Malmesbury)

What survives of the abbey stands on hallowed ground indeed. There was a church here in the seventh century; destroyed by fire in the ninth century, it was immediately rebuilt. It was again destroyed by fire shortly before the Norman Conquest, and rebuilt in the twelfth century. Such hallowed sites must not be left too long unoccupied and here at Malmesbury was the shrine of St Aldhelm himself.

The church built here between 1160 and 1170 was some 240ft long and each transept had a chapel attached to its east side. If the antiquary Leland is to be believed, the spire above the crossing tower surpassed that of Salisbury Cathedral itself, and the tower was balanced by a splendid pair of towers built in the late fourteenth century over the west end of the great nave. Where are those towers today, however? Leland reports that the crossing tower, with its legendary 400ft spire, collapsed about 1530 when he was still a young man; the two west towers collapsed soon after his death in 1552. Soon after the Dissolution virtually everything east of the crossing disintegrated and was vandalised. This is the exact reverse of Dore Abbey.

However, an eminent Wiltshire merchant named William Stumpe built himself a mansion, Abbey House, close by, and conscientiously preserved and restored the nave and presented it to the town of Malmesbury. He was to die in the same year as Leland. Strangely enough, in the basement of his house there is preserved part of the reredorter of the abbey, slanting down towards the river. More of the monastic buildings will be found incorporated in the Bell Hotel, hard by. Formerly known as the Castle Hotel, named after Bishop Roger's castle built in the abbey precinct, it most fittingly incorporates a part of that all-important feature of all well-appointed abbeys: the guest house. There can hardly be, surely, a happier survival of the tradition.

As at Dore Abbey and elsewhere, the monastic buildings lay mainly to the north. The outstanding feature, however, is the incomparable South Porch, more elaborate even than at Kilpeck in Herefordshire. Among the seventy or so individual carvings are God creating Adam and Eve; an Angel offering Eve a distaff; Abraham sacrificing Isaac; Samson rending the lion's jaws; the Magi on their journey to Bethlehem; the Resurrection of Christ; and, for good measure, a man nimbly turning a back-somersault.

Yorkshire (North Riding)

BYLAND ABBEY (Cistercian)

(Between A170 and A19, 8 miles south-east of Thirsk)

As was so often the case, Byland's first steps towards becoming an abbey were tentative and frustrated. An offshoot of Furness Abbey in Lancashire, a small party of monks settled in 1143 on the right bank of the Rye in Ryedale. But Rievaulx Abbey was already established on the left bank of the river, and it was soon found that the monks of each religious house were being disturbed by one another's bells, 'which was not fitting and could by no means be endured'. So, the newcomers were forced to leave. They found a new site on low-lying ground, marshy and unprepossessing, some 5 miles to the south-west. It proved a challenge, and they at once 'began manfully to root out the woods and by long and wide ditches draw off the abundance of water from the marshes; and so, on an ample and worthy site at the foot of the hill of Cambe, at last they built their fair and great church'.

Love as well as skill went into its building. It was paved with green and yellow tiles and even now, after eight centuries, these may still be seen intact in two small chapels in the south transept. Fragments of the capitals from fallen columns reveal that they were picked out in red against a white background. The scale of the church was ambitious : 330ft in length and 140ft across its transepts; and the cloister is 145ft square—larger than that at Rievaulx or at Fountains itself.

But figures such as these, though impressive, are not all-important; often it is the small detail that one remembers longest. For instance, there is a little socket in the upper of two steps leading from the monks' quire into the presbytery: it once held the stem on which was mounted the wooden lectern. Or again: in the north-east corner of the cloister, set in the west wall of the south transept, there are the remains of a cupboard, an offshoot of the library behind it. Here were kept the books which the monks might read as they paced the cloister walks. From it would be fetched the book which the monk on reading-duty would read aloud to his brethren as they ate in silence in the spacious refectory.

Very often it is minor details like these that bring home to one, more even than the remains of the flying buttresses and the splendid arches and clerestories, the way-of-life of the men who constituted these Cistercian communities all those centuries ago.

Yorkshire (North Riding)

EASBY ABBEY (Premonstratensian)

(Off B6271, 1 mile east of Richmond)

The lovely River Swale which has hitherto run eastwards through Swaledale, turns southwards, clear of the fells. About the middle of the twelfth century, the Abbey of St Agatha, as it was long known, was established on the left bank of the river. Because the site was restricted, the layout of the monastic buildings could not absolutely conform to tradition. Easby is particularly interesting because here so many of the 'rules' had to be broken. The abbey church, of which little remains, could not be truly orientated; though the cloister, sacristy, chapter house and frater are all, as usual, on the south side, the abbot's lodgings, the infirmary and the misericord, where aged and ailing monks were permitted certain privileges denied to their brethren, were not only on the north side of the church but accessible through the north transept itself.

As at Shap Abbey in Westmorland, of the same order, the church has survived less well than other buildings. The nave, however, shares with that abbey the distinction of possessing the incised part-circles in its paving that were designed to indicate the exact positions the canons were to take up at the close of their Sunday processional walk.

The most outstanding relic at Easby is, for once, the frater or refectory. It constitutes the whole of the south range; it lacks roof and the floor of the upper storey (though the joist-holes are still to be seen), but the great walls rise almost to their original height. Whether viewed from the exterior or the interior, it is a magnificent edifice. You can still see, in a bay of the south wall, the pulpitum from which the reading-monk read to those at table.

Because the site was not only restricted but sloped considerably, a great deal of ingenuity was called for in the placing of the various monastic buildings, often on different levels. You will notice the unusual shape of the cloister—neither square nor rectangular; the dorter was in the west range, not the usual east, and the warming house too. The reredorter had to be approached through the guests' chamber, because the river, here converted into a mill-race, had to be used for drainage. There are therefore more stairs than was usual, and in more than one case some form of bridge-passage obviously had to be built in order to facilitate communications.

Yorkshire (North Riding)

EGGLESTONE ABBEY (Premonstratensian)

(Off A66, 2 miles south of Barnard Castle)

Like, among others, Tintern Abbey, Egglestone is laid out with its ancillary buildings to the north instead of to the south of the church. It was founded by a group of monks from Easby Abbey in the very last years of the twelfth century but it never attained the size and prosperity of its mother church, and very soon suffered the indignity of an official inquiry as to whether it should be relegated to the status of a priory. It was not; but it remained poor and without influence throughout its history. It was unlucky in that it lay in the path of roving baronial forces in perpetual and swaying conflict with the Scots. Discipline, as with the Cluniacs at Castle Acre, became lax, and the small and struggling house was constantly in trouble.

Misfortune dogged the place even after the common misfortune of the Dissolution. In 1548 it became the property of one Robert Strelley, who ruthlessly took material from one part to improve or enlarge another that he was already adapting for his personal use as a residence. More than two centuries later its fabric was still being cannibalised, this time for the paving of the stable yard at neighbouring Rokeby Hall. However, as at Shap Abbey, a later conscience was pricked, and such stone as was still serviceable was returned to the abbey and reinstalled *in situ* wherever possible.

The north wall of the early thirteenth-century nave and the later south wall, and parts of the presbytery walls, still stand, some of them almost to their original height. The great east window is a very remarkable and virtually unique example of the work of its period, about the middle of the thirteenth century; its four great mullions divide its space with a starkness, even a severity, that evokes admiration.

There is no west tower, but it is believed that there was formerly a crossing tower: there are signs of this in the masonry of the walls that would have carried it. Where is it, then? It seems that once again we are indebted to Robert Strelley for his malign influence on the site; it is probable, if not certain, that he had it dismantled because it interfered with the light he demanded for the residence he had so ruthlessly adapted from the canons' dorter and the chapter house that had constituted the greater part of the north range of the monastic buildings.

Yorkshire (West Riding)

FOUNTAINS ABBEY (Cistercian)

(Between A61 and B6265, 3 miles south-west of Ripon)

The most splendid surviving example of a Cistercian monastery, and also the most beautifully sited. It bestrides a half-mile reach of Skelldale, between the quarried face of Rye Bank and the well-wooded south side of the river. Here were its 20 acres of orchards, its fish-ponds, its bakehouse and malthouse, its smithy and wheelwright's shop and many other ancillary buildings.

It is the supreme example of a great tree grown from a tiny seed, for its founders were a handful of dissident Benedictines determined to establish a more austere way of life. Here they created it. Late in December 1132, they found a site 'uninhabited for all the centuries back, thick set with thorns and fit rather to be the lair of wild beasts than the home of human beings'. Their first home was an undercut rockshelf; in the spring they moved out into the shelter of a great elm—the site of which is still marked at the eastern end of what was to become a 70 acre precinct—and built a tiny chapel. Because clear water sprang from the rocks that had sheltered them, they named their new abode Fountains.

The magnificent remains of their abbey—the now roofless church, the cloister and chapter house, the kitchen, the warming room, the infirmary, west range, reredorters and other named portions—are all dominated by the glorious seven-storey tower that rises 170ft from the end of the north transept, the creation of the great Abbot Huby in the fifteenth century.

Less spectacular, but in its way even more interesting, and quite unique, is canalising by the twelfth-century monks of the Skell's waters into four parallel stone tunnels 90yd in length and passing beneath many of the major buildings. Thus the kitchens had 'running water', as did some of the latrines, which were ingeniously designed to be served by this natural drainage system.

Another remarkable feature of Fountains is the 22-bay, 300ft long lay-brothers' refectory and stores, the largest in this or any other European country. The feature emphasises the abbey's greatness: in substance, in dignity, in importance and in influence. At the Dissolution, Fountains was the richest Cistercian prize to fall into the hands of the avaricious King Henry VIII.

Yorkshire (North Riding)

GUISBOROUGH PRIORY (Augustinian)

(In the grounds of Guisborough Hall, 5 miles south-west of Saltburn)

Do not be put off if you are told that 'There's only one fragment of it left'. This may be fairly true, but that 'fragment' still standing is among the noblest surviving examples of late-thirteenth-century ecclesiastical architecture in the whole country. The east end of the presbytery still stands to its original height of almost a hundred feet; it is pierced by one of the most beautifully proportioned east windows in existence: 56ft high and 23ft wide. It occupies almost the whole span of this east wall, flanked on either side by smaller windows and grouped buttresses of perfect design. The priory is well worth a visit for this feature alone; its lovely setting, curtained to the south by the great curve of magnificent lime trees, again more than justifies a visit.

The priory was founded by Robert de Brus—an ancestor of Robert the Bruce—early in the twelfth century, and immediately endowed with no less than 10,000 acres of good Yorkshire land; building proceeded apace, but disaster was round the corner. On 16 May 1289, a metal-worker with two boy assistants was repairing the lead sheeting on the church roof. His task completed, he descended his ladders, leaving the boys to clear up after him. One of them upset a 'pan of live coles' that had been used for soldering the joints. Scared, the two boys scrambled back down the ladders, swearing one another to secrecy. Meanwhile, a roof joist caught fire; the fire, fanned by a strong wind, immediately spread. The monks below were at Mass. Suddenly a wide gap appeared in the roof and molten lead began to pour down on them like a stream of lava. The whole roof was soon in flames and caved in; the flames spread throughout the church and it was burned to the ground. With it vanished precious relics, chalices, vestments and the whole famous collection of rare volumes amassed by a succession of dedicated priors. Only the south and west walls of the nave escaped; the whole of the rest of the great church had to be rebuilt from the foundations.

Two and a half centuries later, after the Dissolution, a second wave of damage befell the priory. As a result, only one corner of the south transept and the west wall of the cellarer's range survive—apart, that is to say, from the breathtakingly beautiful 'fragment', the superb east end of the presbytery.

Yorkshire (North Riding)

JERVAULX ABBEY (Cistercian)

(On A6108, 4 miles south-east of Leyburn)

Standing on the left bank of the Ure just to the east of the point where Wensleydale opens out into low-lying terrain, Jervaulx is an offshoot of Byland Abbey, some 20 miles to the east. It was founded by the authorities there in the mid-twelfth century but not on its present site. The story of its siting has a touch of the myth, but in a context such as this, a myth is not difficult to accept on its face value.

Accompanied by twelve monks, Abbot John de Kingston set off on foot from Byland for Wensleydale. Dusk overtook them, the forest was dense and mist descended from the fells; soon they were lost. They prayed for guidance, and the Virgin Mary, with the Holy Child in her arms, appeared to them. 'Ye are late of Byland,' she said, 'but now ye shall be of Yorevale.' To this day 'Yore' is a recognised pronunciation of the river shown as Ure; the name Jervaulx echoes the name Yorevale. The monks rejoiced, and proceeded to establish themselves on the level bank of the Ure. They prospered, were granted rights of mining and territory well up the valley to the west. Year by year they enlarged their monastery; but they were still subject to Byland.

The layout of their monastery can still be clearly seen, though few of the buildings stand to any appreciable height. An altar in one chapel built into the north transept is remarkable for the preservation of the five crosses incised in it. Another modest feature is of particular interest: it is a recess in a column at the foot of the stone steps from the monks' dorter which contained the holy water that was sprinkled by the monks as they processed into the quire. Enough remains of the monastic buildings generally to indicate that it was spaciously designed. The church must have been nearly 300ft in length, though all too little of it remains; the monks' dorter extended right over the large chapter house. Jervaulx was built with pride as well as skill. This is emphasised by the number of masons' marks still in evidence, the individual 'signatures' with which master masons stamped the stonework for which they were responsible. There are no fewer than fifteen of these, and this reveals the strength of the expert labour force that was engaged there in the twelfth, thirteen and fourteenth centuries.

Yorkshire (East Riding)

KIRKHAM PRIORY (Augustinian)

(Off A64, 5 miles south-west of Malton)

This priory is on a beautiful site, on the left bank of the serpentining River Derwent. A legend, which may well be truth, is associated with its founding in or about 1122. The Lord of Helmsley (a name that has rung down the centuries in this part of Yorkshire), a man named Walter l'Espec, saw his only son killed when out riding with him in the water-meadows. In memory of his beloved child, he founded an Augustinian priory on the exact spot. Less than ten years later he founded Rievaulx Abbey, this time for the Cistercian Order. This may partly account for the restlessness within the priory in its early years which resulted in a number of the monks receiving permission to depart to another foundation. Those who remained true, together with later adherents, consolidated Kirkham as a true and loyal house of Augustinian (or Black) Canons.

Of its buildings today, the finest surviving relic is the gatehouse, whose north front is one of the most beautiful examples of thirteenth-century design. The magnificent gateway is surmounted by a gable which in turn is surmounted by a high, buttressed wall pierced by two ornate windows framing a niche containing statuary. On one side of it, boldly carved, is St George and the Dragon; on the other, David and Goliath. It is very rare to find a gatehouse to an abbey or priory, so richly ornamented.

Another of the all too few surviving relics is the gateway leading from the south-west corner of the cloister into the frater. Less huge, less ornate, than the other, it is nevertheless an impressive piece of Romanesque construction. Near it, just outside the frater itself, is a very fine example of a feature common to all these buildings but rarely so beautiful in conception, or so well preserved. This is the canons' lavatorium where they washed their hands before entering the frater. It is a trough (formerly lead lined) through which clear water constantly flowed.

Of the church itself little of the earliest work remains save the south wall of the nave and part of the south transept. In 1180 these walls were deliberately thickened from 4ft to 6ft, which accounts for their survival. South and east of the church and cloister, the ancillary buildings lie in a curious curve as though to enclose the chapter house, the quire and the presbytery.

Yorkshire (West Riding)

MONK BRETTON PRIORY (Benedictine)

(On the eastern outskirts of Barnsley)

This was a foundation of the Cluniac Order in 1154. Before the end of the next century, strangely enough, it had become, as it was to remain, Benedictine. The fact hints at trouble, and certainly its early history reveals that there was, throughout the reign of the early priors, continuous trouble. There was friction between this and the older Cluniac house at neighbouring Pontefract; the precinct was barred time and again to other Cluniac priors who, officially, had the right of access and entry. One such prior actually sent an armed party to storm and occupy Monk Bretton. Eventually an appeal was made to the Archbishop of York and, in 1281, the priory became Benedictine.

It still underwent changes of fortune, however, including a great fire which destroyed much of its property, and there was insufficient money to rebuild as the monks would have wished. At the Dissolution it suffered as other establishments did: the lead was stripped from its roof and the bells and other valuable metal-work was removed and sent to the king. Nor did the ravaging end there. The north aisle of the nave, with its arches and columns, was dismantled and used in the building of neighbouring Wentworth Church; soon afterwards the prior's lodging and the frater itself were turned into a residence for the Earl of Shrewsbury's son.

Today, parts of the north and south transepts can be seen, and there is a particularly interesting feature in the north wall of the twelfth-century presbytery. It is a recess in the stonework which was almost certainly of great importance. An early chronicler records (writing of a similar feature in St Augustine's Abbey, Canterbury) that 'many relics of the Saints were hidden in various parts of the church, to be found when it shall please God and His Saints'.

The frater here is outstanding; though not as fine as that at Easby, it does have a notably fine window in its south wall. Comparable with this, in interest at any rate, is the east wall of the prior's chamber. It contains an unusually well-preserved fireplace, with a tapering hood above its massive lintel and, a charming touch, a moulded lamp-bracket at each end of the lintel, carved in one piece. One can visualise the prior, privileged to have a fire to himself, sitting there and reading from some holy book from the library on the other side of the cloister.

Yorkshire (North Riding)

MOUNT GRACE PRIORY (Carthusian)

(Off A172, 10 miles north-east of Northallerton)

Only nine Carthusian monasteries, or Charterhouses, were ever established in England; because of their extreme austerity they lacked the attractiveness of the other orders. This was the eighth to be founded. In 1398 the Duke of Surrey selected for it a lonely site near Ingleby, on the western foothills of the Cleveland Hills. Isolation, for the Carthusians, was a vital prerequisite; they demanded isolation not only from the world outside but from one another within the precinct. For this reason the layout of a charterhouse differed fundamentally from that of all other orders. Nowhere is this better illustrated than here at Mount Grace.

Its central feature (as always) is an enormous cloister, lozenge-shaped rather than rectangular, with one side of 272ft and the others of 231ft. Around three sides, set close together but insulated by high, thick walls, are some twenty cells, each exactly 27ft square and set in an angle of its own garden, where the occupant worked for part of each long day. More hermit than monk, he lived, worked, meditated, prayed alone. Only on certain feast days did the monks eat communally; otherwise they ate alone, their sparse food being brought to each cell by a lay-brother and served through a skew-set hatch so that neither man could see the other. There was no communal reredorter, but each cell had its own private garderobe, or latrine, and water was piped to each cell individually from a conduit-house fed by a spring. Each monk had razor, pen and ink, needle and thread, a thin robe and a shirt made of some coarse material 'to irritate and tame the flesh'.

Since there was little ritual, the church is modestly proportioned and simple to the point of severity. The community met there only once daily, and always without speaking to one another. There is a small nave, with two small, transept-like chapels beneath a fine early fifteenth-century tower at the crossing; eastwards, only the north wall of the quire and presbytery survive to any height. One of the cells has been fully reconstructed but there are few other surviving buildings. The remains of kitchen and guest house, and the prior's own cell which, like a few of the other cells, was built against the wall of the church: that is all that can be seen today. All in all, it is certainly the grouping of these individual cells round the huge cloister that excites curiosity and commands interest in the visitor to this most unusual type of religious house.

Yorkshire (North Riding)

RIEVAULX ABBEY (Cistercian)

(Off B1257, 3 miles north-west of Helmsley)

Among its less well known claims to distinction—even in one respect uniqueness—this is the only religious house whose founding and earliest development led to the deliberate re-routing of a river in its own valley. Established in 1131 on the left bank of the Rye in Ryedale, it was quickly seen that more land would be required. Three successive grants were made by the landowners to the first abbots permitting them to deflect the course of the river and thus gain more level land, and after three decades the abbey was so large that it 'swarmed with 140 monks and 500 lay-brethren, like a hive with bees'.

The great church is most unusual in that, owing to the lie of the land, with a western-falling slope, it had to be orientated not east-west but south-north. It was the first large Cistercian church to be built in Britain, and can claim to be older than any other still standing even in France. Though its twelfth-century nave is austere almost to severity, the remaining bays and tiers of arcading in the later quire and presbytery are more ornate and rank among the finest examples of English-Gothic known. The discerning eye can pick out the successive stages of building, for the later masons used a whiter, more finely-grained sandstone than the earlier. Dominating these remains is the superb arch, all that survives of the crossing tower: it soars 75ft above presbytery and quire.

Because of the slope down towards the river, this could not be used (as it was, most notably, at Fountains) for direct supplies to kitchens, lavatories and drainage-systems; instead, water was piped from springs on the hillside to the east, collected in a so-called conduit-house, and then ingeniously distributed about the buildings. You can see the stone channels through which it was conveyed, for instance, beneath the refectory to the reredorters and thence to its outfall in the river, well clear of the abbey precinct.

West of the fine chapter house, with its unusual arcaded apse, may be seen the remains of the long, narrow parlour. The name indicates its purpose: here, and here only, the monks might 'hold parley', or speak with one another; absolute silence was imposed, of course, in the adjacent cloister walks where they meditated or read the prescribed books from the library adjacent to the south transept.

Yorkshire (West Riding)

ROCHE ABBEY (Cistercian)

(Off A634, 8 miles south-east of Rotherham)

The site of this abbey, like that of another and greater Cistercian house, Fountains Abbey, is a valley. A stream flows along it and (again as at Fountains) the abbey buildings bestride this. Two neighbouring landowners, Richard de Bully and Richard son of Turgis, bequeathed land jointly to the monks: one the right bank, the other the left bank of the stream, leaving it to them to decide how to make the best use of this somewhat unusual site. It has another feature in common with Fountains Abbey: it is bounded to the north by a stretch of steep, rocky cliff, and it is from this that it derives its name. The gatehouse, at the north-west corner of the precinct, the ground floor of which is unusually well preserved, was built hard up against this.

The monks laid out the church itself, with its cloister, chapter house and lay-brothers' dorter, on the north bank of the stream. The monks' dorter and the all-important frater, by tradition were situated south of these main buildings, and because of the stream that crossed their line the south ends of these buildings overlapped and had therefore to be carried across the stream on a succession of low-slung, massive bridges. The line of these can be traced, for the monks' reredorter, as was usual, had to have an active drain, and the seats were placed along the south wall of this building in order to be served thereby. Further across the south bank still was the abbot's lodging and, adjacent to it, his kitchen and the lay-brothers' infirmary.

Of the church, the most impressive remains are the two transepts, whose walls still stand almost to their original height; the nave, however, is today little more than breast height. Unlike some abbey churches—Shap for example—it seems to have been built entire in the second half of the twelfth century, instead of at two different periods. From what remains of the frater, it must have been less cold than some, for it lay exactly between the warming house and the kitchen that served it. Oddly, the daïs occupied by the senior monks is at the south end, over the stream and remote from the comfort of the hot air flowing across the north end. The kitchen had, like that at Fountains, an immense central hearth and chimney, with an open hearth on one face, and smaller hearths and ovens on the three other faces.

Yorkshire (North Riding)

WHITBY ABBEY (Benedictine)

(On East Cliff, ½ mile east of the town)

It would hardly be an exaggeration to state that no Benedictine (or indeed any other religious house, not even Lindisfarne Priory) is more spectacularly, more nobly sited than this. It surmounts the great East Cliff on which a Saxon monastery is known to have stood more than twelve centuries ago, and on which, almost certainly, a beacon for shipping was installed in late Roman times. The site is exposed to every wind of heaven (and was actually shelled by German warships in 1914): it is therefore small wonder that so little of the early thirteenth-century abbey buildings have survived even as well as they have done. So, why this most unpromising site? It has been suggested that it was deliberately chosen by the earliest monks (in AD 657) rather as the hermits of Egypt and elsewhere in the Middle East chose deserts for their self-imposed isolation.

What does survive today would be impressive even on a lowlier site: the majestic north and east walls of the presbytery, for instance, and the splendid north aisle of the nave. The north transept which, in spite of being inevitably the most exposed portion of the abbey to the prevailing north-east wind, still stands almost to its original height. Within the storm-battered shell, the clustered shafts and richly moulded arches, trefoiled and quatrefoiled, the detail work of the foliage capitals, the shapely, pointed clerestory windows, all survive to delight the discerning eye.

Astonishing that so much of this should have survived so many centuries of onslaught by wind and weather on England's most bitterly exposed sea-coast. Astonishing, too, to realise that the tower above the crossing collapsed only as recently as 1830, nearly six centuries after it was built. Like the campanile in the Piazza San Marco, Venice some seventy years later, it subsided entirely without warning on a calm day in late June.

Though the church roof was stripped of its lead immediately after the Dissolution, the abbey was not cannibalised for its building-stone quite as ruthlessly as were many other doomed religious houses; this may have been because its value as a landmark to coastal shipping continued to be recognised. Thus a site once used as a signal-station by the Romans preserves, even to this day, something of its value in that respect—quite apart from its spectacular beauty as a medieval Parthenon on an English acropolis.

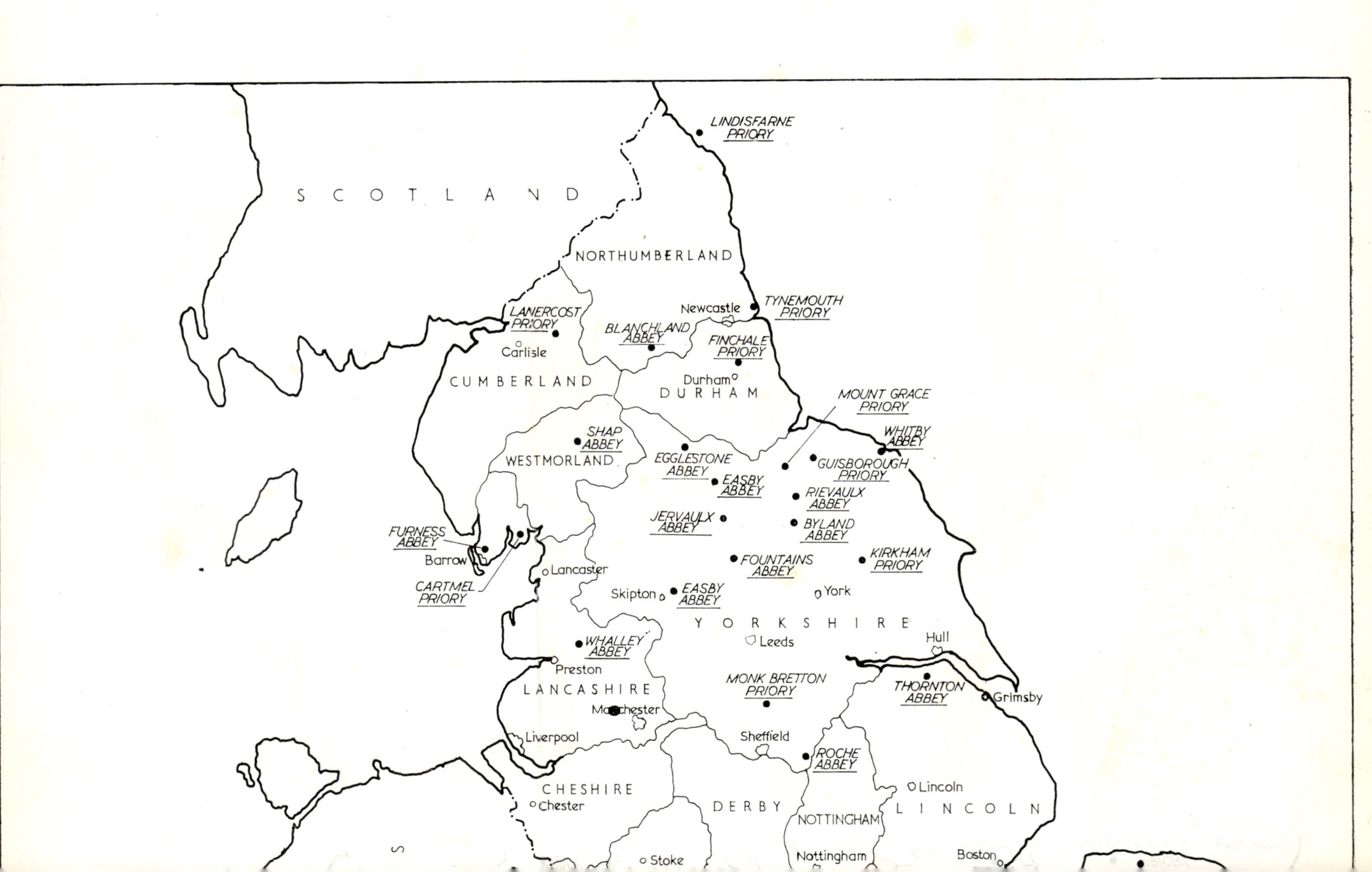

SCOTLAND
NORTHUMBERLAND
LINDISFARNE PRIORY
TYNEMOUTH PRIORY
Newcastle
LANERCOST PRIORY
BLANCHLAND ABBEY
FINCHALE PRIORY
Carlisle
CUMBERLAND
Durham
DURHAM
MOUNT GRACE PRIORY
WHITBY ABBEY
SHAP ABBEY
WESTMORLAND
EGGLESTONE ABBEY
EASBY ABBEY
GUISBOROUGH PRIORY
RIEVAULX ABBEY
JERVAULX ABBEY
BYLAND ABBEY
FURNESS ABBEY
Barrow
CARTMEL PRIORY
Lancaster
FOUNTAINS ABBEY
KIRKHAM PRIORY
Skipton
EASBY ABBEY
York
YORKSHIRE
Leeds
Hull
WHALLEY ABBEY
Preston
LANCASHIRE
MONK BRETTON PRIORY
THORNTON ABBEY
Grimsby
Manchester
Liverpool
Sheffield
ROCHE ABBEY
CHESHIRE
Chester
DERBY
NOTTINGHAM
Lincoln
LINCOLN
Stoke
Nottingham
Boston
S

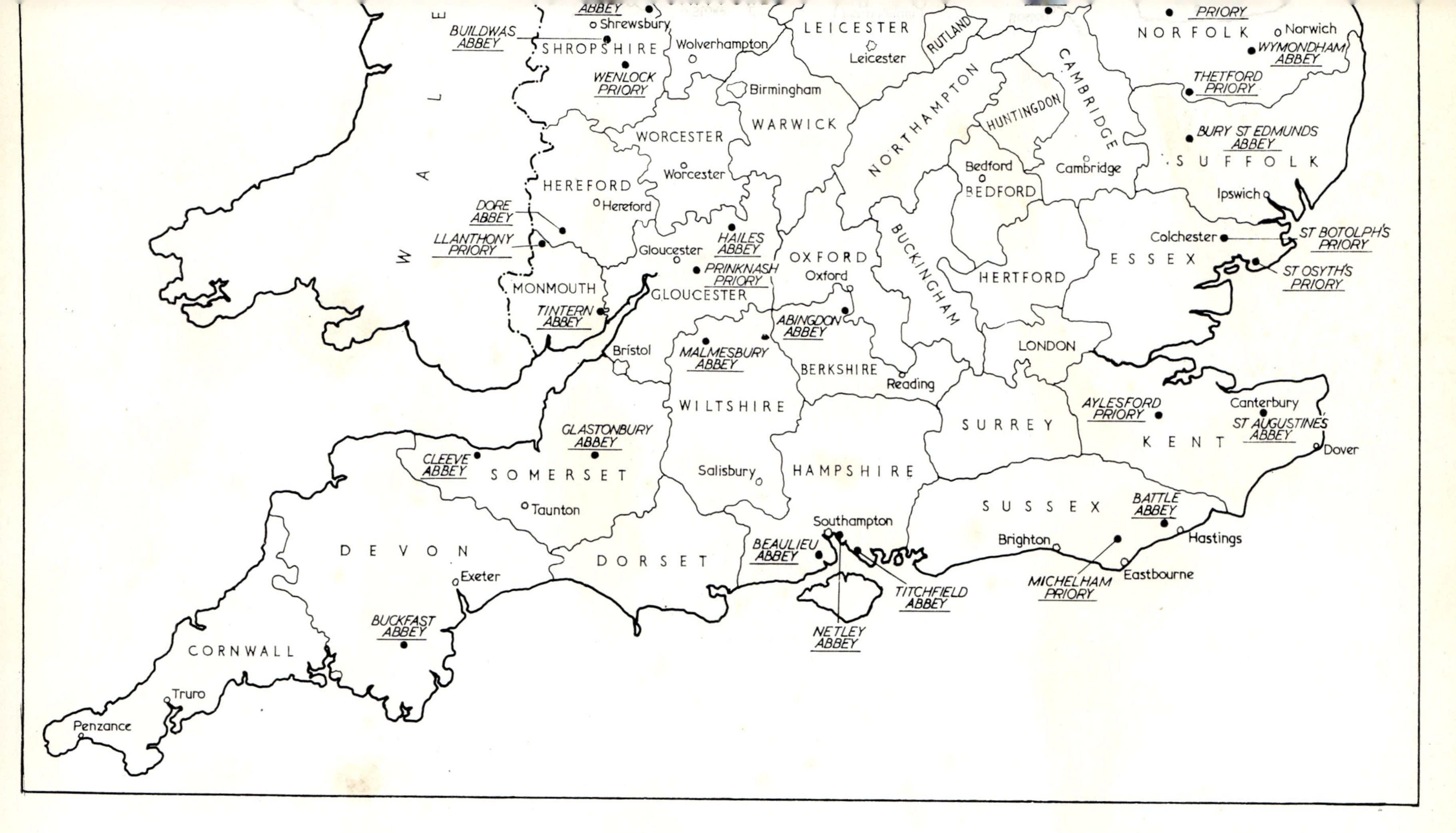

BUILDWAS ABBEY
Shrewsbury
SHROPSHIRE
WENLOCK PRIORY
Wolverhampton
LEICESTER
Leicester
RUTLAND
NORFOLK
Norwich
WYMONDHAM ABBEY
THETFORD PRIORY
Birmingham
WARWICK
WORCESTER
Worcester
NORTHAMPTON
HUNTINGDON
CAMBRIDGE
Cambridge
Bedford
BEDFORD
BURY ST EDMUNDS ABBEY
SUFFOLK
Ipswich
W A L E
HEREFORD
Hereford
DORE ABBEY
LLANTHONY PRIORY
HAILES ABBEY
Gloucester
PRINKNASH PRIORY
GLOUCESTER
OXFORD
Oxford
BUCKINGHAM
HERTFORD
ESSEX
Colchester
ST BOTOLPH'S PRIORY
ST OSYTH'S PRIORY
MONMOUTH
TINTERN ABBEY
ABINGDON ABBEY
Bristol
MALMESBURY ABBEY
BERKSHIRE
Reading
LONDON
WILTSHIRE
SURREY
AYLESFORD PRIORY
Canterbury
ST AUGUSTINE'S ABBEY
KENT
Dover
GLASTONBURY ABBEY
CLEEVE ABBEY
SOMERSET
Taunton
Salisbury
HAMPSHIRE
SUSSEX
BATTLE ABBEY
Southampton
Brighton
Hastings
DEVON
Exeter
DORSET
BEAULIEU ABBEY
TITCHFIELD ABBEY
NETLEY ABBEY
MICHELHAM PRIORY
Eastbourne
BUCKFAST ABBEY
CORNWALL
Truro
Penzance

GLOSSARY

Aumbry	Wall recess to hold sacramental vessels
Chapter House	Room in which monastic business was daily transacted
Cloister	Four-sided area consisting of garth surrounded by (usually) covered walk; ordinarily situated on the south side of the nave
Collation Seat	Seat on cloister walk adjacent to the nave, in which the prior or abbot sat and watched the brethren reading or at meditation in the walks
Crossing	Area of church where its west-east axis is crossed by the south-north transepts; usually surmounted by a tower
Dorter	The monks' dormitory, usually on upper floor of the east range
Frater	The monks' dining-hall, or refectory
Galilee	A porch extending the full width of the west entrance to the church
Lavatorium	Trough with running water, adjacent to the frater, where the monks washed their hands; usually in a corner of the cloister walk
Lay Brethren	Monks not in Holy Orders, mainly employed in manual labour
Misericord	A small frater, usually adjacent to the infirmary, in which the sick or very elderly brethren were permitted dishes not served to their fellows. Also an elaborate carved shelf on the under side of the seat in a monk's stall
Presbytery	The east portion of the church, containing the altar
Pulpitum	A stone pulpit-chair inset in the frater wall, often reached by steps, for the use of the monk reading aloud at meal times
Quire (or Choir)	Area between the nave and the presbytery containing the monks' stalls
Reredorter	A building adjacent to the dorter, usually over the main drain and fitted as a latrine, flushed by running water in a channel. It corresponds to the garderobe of the medieval castle, by which name it is sometimes known
Slype	A passageway across a range of monastic buildings
Warming Room	The only room, other than the kitchen, in which the brethren might have access to a fire. Known also as Warming House or as the Calefactory